SO YOU WANT TO OWN A SUBWAY FRANCHISE?

A Decade In the Restaurant Business

By
Dylan Randall and Shayne Randall

Strategic Book Group

Strategic Book Group
P.O. Box 333
Durham CT 06422
www.StrategicBookClub.com

ISBN 978-1-60976-427-2

Printed in the United States of America

PREFACE

The thought of owning your own business can be invigorating and exciting. Controlling one's own destiny is a concept most of us thrive on because, in many instances, it captures the ambitions inside us that are in danger of remaining dormant. When those ambitions become realistically achievable, we are motivated by their potential. In the past thirty years, the popularity of franchising has risen as people are becoming more curious about the concept as it has become a more attainable dream. We are not thinking about finding jobs for life as we used to. Goals are measured in a smaller time frame knowing that career paths might change. As loyalties between employees and their bosses weakened, job security was not a sought after goal. A more cutthroat employer emerged and a more risk-oriented job force took shape.

In 1925, at sixteen years of age, my grandfather, Fenwick Randall, took a summer job at Graselli Chemicals, a company in Toronto's east end. His father, Ken Randall, a notable professional hockey player, was quick to advise his son to take a permanent position with the company if it was offered to him at the end of the summer. My grandfather, who was an excellent hockey player himself, extinguished any dreams of following his old man into the NHL and took a steady job at Graselli knowing that such a solid occupation was hard to come by. He stayed with the company, which later became C.I.L., until he retired in 1976. Back in 1925, a job was the most valuable currency a person had. Acquiring an occupation and keeping it was your life's goal. Today it is a much different reality dictated by a "survival of the fittest" business environment. Consequently, individuals have emerged who are willing to take calculated risks.

Shayne Randall, my father, is someone who spent much of his business life taking the kind of risks that would have been too daunting in his father's time. He had many careers, the success of each reliant on his ability to take risks. At the age of fifty-eight, a decade removed from any quantifiable business achievements, he took one of his biggest gambles when he bought a Subway restaurant without any previous experience in the food industry. After ten years as a franchisee, it is fair to say that his risk paid off in spades. Franchising returned him to the millionaire status he once enjoyed in the seventies and eighties.

The telling of our family's journey in the restaurant business, which began in 2000, is intended to answer many of the questions posed when considering the opportunity of owning a franchise. The information contained herein will provide a history and analysis of a man and his family partaking in a ten-year partnership with Subway. It is a story filled with insights into how we were successful, missteps to avoid, and details an experience that should reveal whether Subway is the right franchise for you. It specifically explains how Subway conducts itself in Eastern and Northern Ontario (ENO) and describes relationships with Subway World Headquarters (Subway HQ). If you are at a career crossroads, this narrative might point you towards becoming a franchisee, or you may conclude that your career should go in another direction. Either way, it will be time well spent.

DYLAN RANDALL

TABLE OF CONTENTS

PART I

ENTERING THE FRAY

Since I spent a lot of time baking bread, slicing tomatoes, and interacting with customers when I was in my late teens and early twenties, I certainly learned all the tasks that would entail working at and eventually owning a Subway restaurant. And of course, even when I was young, I reeked of that inescapable Subway-like odor of a food shop.

Working for my parents was different than working for a stranger in that I couldn't deceive my parents in the same way most other employees would. On the other hand, I liked that I could take any food I wanted without it being considered stealing and that I knew I wasn't going to get fired. Family involvement was essential to the success of the stores my family owned from 2000-2009. Without his wife and sons working with him, it would have been very difficult for my dad to assemble a staff he could trust and maintain over a significant period of time. When you're paying people minimum wage, they aren't imagining the job as a career or as necessarily an important part of their life that requires great effort or scrutiny. However, if your family is the main part of the staff the proper care is usually taken. Employee theft is virtually eliminated when family minds the till.

Born in 1981, I barely remember the eighties, but from what I recall, my family had money. How much I could never quantify. My buddy Luke always had the newest video games, and his mom kept their fridge stocked fuller than any other kid's on our street. Naturally, I would head over to his house, wishing my mom would do as Luke's and spoil my brothers and me the same way. For all I knew, Luke's family was better off than mine. It wasn't until the mid-nineties that I realized how much money my dad really had and how much he suddenly didn't have. It was a strange morning when my parents told me he had lost his biggest source of income, Gateway Manufacturing, a company that recycled photocopiers. I was initially indifferent to the news because until that point, I never had reason to worry about my livelihood or understand what that word even meant. In the ensuing years, with what he told me about his past business experiences, his friends recollections of him, and my added maturity, I was able to put into context how we lived during the those times and ultimately his ability as an entrepreneur.

In the seventies and eighties, my father sold Savin photocopiers and franchised the company across eastern Ontario until it grew to where he could open other businesses connected to the selling of photocopiers. He started a leasing company, and he started a company that recycled copiers and re-sold them. They were all successful. Times were prosperous up until he ran into a complicated situation with the bank and the city of Peterborough that ended with him going bankrupt. Savin and the bank manipulated him for a lot of money, and he retaliated by suing both parties. He settled with Savin for a fraction of what he was owed because he was broke at the time. Eighteen years later, the lawsuit with the city is still going on.

While representing Savin/Ricoh, Shayne won dealer of the year several times. The company treated him well all the way through even though the end was a bit ugly. He would tell anyone that, overall, they were good to him. They should have been. He was making them a lot of money. The reason I am explaining his record in business prior to Subway is to contrast how both companies treated him. One would assume that with all his success over the past few decades—in more complex ventures—he would be embraced with open arms to run a small business like a Subway restaurant. Subway describes itself in its franchise concept as an "easy-to-run operation," with "low investment, low overhead, and a simple operation (no cooking involved) alternative to what other quick-serve restaurants are offering." Subway observes all franchisees under the same set of parameters. The adherence of franchisees to the Subway Operations Manual and subsequent performance would be the standard of measurement that would determine whether or not a franchisee was successful. In our case, had we worked on strengthening our relationship with our development agent (who presides over the territory of eastern and northern Ontario (ENO)), our journey would have been much less stressful.

In 1999, after almost a decade of wandering through a multitude of meaningless positions, Shayne decided he wanted to try something totally and literally fresh at the age of fifty-eight. He decided the "family" (he viewed it as a family adventure while I simply saw it as a job at the time) should own a Subway restaurant, although none of us had ever worked in the food industry. A Subway restaurant is a small venture that does not have the worries of selling liquor or having to grill anything. The operation required a fridge, freezer, proofer, oven, and microwave. That's all you need. It seemed simpler than running any other kind of restaurant. The business formula that Subway has cultivated over the years is brilliant in its resourcefulness and simplicity. It does not require much formal education or supreme intelligence. You just need to follow the Subway blueprint. Put in the effort and long hours, especially at the start, and your store will become an efficient and prolific moneymaker.

Subway is an attractive franchise to many because it is affordable and appears to be capable of a good return on investment. However, you cannot succeed as an absentee owner. If this is a business you are looking to run on the side, while putting most of your energy elsewhere, think again. The store needs your attention. You will have to micromanage at many points because minimum wage employees require guidance and motivation on an ongoing basis. The staff's efficiency will never be optimal unless you are there to keep them on their toes. Shayne and I would discover this and much more through our experiences over the following ten years.

SELECTING YOUR FRANCHISE

It's important to look back in time when making your next business career decision. When analyzing your past successes and failures, make a list of both. Use the "what you did well" list as an outline of your strengths and the "what you did badly" list to outline your weaknesses. This will become the guideline for making a further list of franchises that might suit you. With literally hundreds to choose from, this exercise will narrow down your choices.

Next, decide what franchises fall into your comfort range. For example, if you are not technically proficient you could eliminate a Handyman franchise. Circle a franchise on the list that fits your strengths. If you like working outdoors, consider Weedman. Put yourself into a situation where you can utilize your strengths, and you will be more successful. After all, you'll be doing this for a while.

After thirty-five years of running various owner-operated businesses, my father searched for a franchise that would stimulate his interest and perhaps put him in a segment that he had not been in before. Having a large family that would be able to get involved in a daily operation, he sought a franchise opportunity that would allow immediate participation by family members. With children ranging from twelve to eighteen years old, something close to home would be appealing. He wanted something where his investment could be reclaimed in three to five years while allowing for an exit sale within ten years.

He asked himself:

- Could I expand?
- Was a workforce readily available?
- Was it a growing industry?
- Was the franchise name of value?
- What was the geographical marketing area proposed?
- Was the customer base young?
- Was the geographical area becoming more populated?
- Was it a business that would not become dull and mundane?

There are many more criteria he considered. His health, energy level, work hour limits, safety, competition, government restriction, integrity of the franchisor, product limitations, franchise language and interpretation, royalties, involvement of suppliers, workforce availability and training, reporting requirements, compliance issues (involving the government, the health department, and the franchisor), marketing opportunities, income statement analysis, and franchise purchase comparisons and analysis. The most compelling factor would be whether an existing operational franchise was available or whether a store construction was necessary.

Using the aforementioned criteria, he set out to search for a franchise opportunity. He only had $60,000 in start-up cash, and his search window was three to six months. He had narrowed down the investigation to three different kinds of businesses. A sports related business, business consulting, and restaurant were the sectors he was most interested in.

We lived in Peterborough, Ontario, a community of 80,000 people located within one hundred miles of Toronto. He was mobile enough that even a big city opportunity wasn't out of the question.

He researched a golf franchise situation. It was a start-up requiring the construction of a store in our community. The cash required would be $250,000 with an additional $250,000 in bank financing. This was a gigantic leap of faith in that the franchisor had been established less than ten years, and at least $1.5 million in yearly sales was required to break even. Return on the original investment was five to seven years at best. An exit strategy was difficult to discern.

The next analysis was for a Tim Horton's franchise, a household name in Canada. It required extensive capital ($750,000 minimum) and an extensive store construction. Because of the brand name strength, sale increases would be rapid. There was at least a five-year window for return on investment. Furthermore, with the restrictions of the franchisor, a resale would be complicated and return on the original investment would be minimal. An exit strategy was hard to envision with that franchise also.

In a sixty-day period, Shayne analyzed almost fifty franchises. The conclusion seemed to be that the best chance of success would lie with an existing operation. The search was narrowed down to the following parameters:

An existing business

- One with a need for new energy with new management
- An investment of $250,000 or less
- Sales flat lining but with upside
- Good brand name recognition
- A location with the promise of future growth
- A reasonable lease
- A workforce that was available
- A business that was conducive to a family run operation

As he wandered through the "franchise jungle" and discussed the opportunities, a theme emerged and many of the would-be franchise opportunities begged the question, "Was I buying a job?" The answer is no. You are investing in a business. After making the choice to become your own boss, you need to focus on being the toughest one you've ever had. Becoming an entrepreneur begins when you seize an opportunity, embrace it, and strive to fulfill its promise. In my mind, franchising can be that opportunity, but if it doesn't get your heart pumping, it might not be the right one for you.

DUE DILIGENCE

In late 1999, Shayne spotted a small advertisement in a local newspaper, "Number One Franchise for sale. Reasonable investment, local business." He contacted the owner who explained that he was selling the last of three Subway stores that he had started in the early 90s. They met, and after several meetings, Shayne was able to perform a thorough analysis of the business. His small business background was useful in breaking down income statements and, more importantly, creating and projecting future income statements as they would pertain to this operation.

The restaurant was located in Bridgenorth, a small village of 1500 residents on a very busy thoroughfare, adjacent to Lake Chemong. Located on a main traffic artery that runs from Peterborough to various northerly locations, Bridgenorth served as the gateway to the Kawartha Lakes, a popular summer holiday destination. The store's sales over the previous two years had peaked at $250,000 yearly—$5,000 per week. At first glance, even projecting a 20% net profit seemed like hardly enough income for a family of six. The summer business was brisk but the weekly sales dipped to under $4,000 during the winter, creating very little cash flow during that period.

However, there were many positives to consider. The car traffic count indicated that potential customers were driving by the door. After visiting the store during lunch and other key times, Shayne deduced that an injection of positive management energy could turn around what appeared to be a sullen and negative staff. New enthusiasm would bring back disgruntled customers who had been turned off by poor customer service, and that same infusion of energy would attract new patrons. There were no other fast food competitors in the area, and Subway was an up and coming name in the industry. The current owner was an absentee, and, as a result, his young staff had become undisciplined and was turning customers away. But the community was growing. There was a definite upside for sales in this area, which was an important prerequisite in Shayne's criteria. He calculated that he could double sales in three to five years. The traffic and local dynamic would help create this growth. A family run operation and a fresh marketing impetus would ensure sales targets were met, and with family supplying much of the labour content, it could be profitable. The seller's terms were as follows.

- A price of $100,000
- A share sale of the company and its assets
- There would be no debt or liabilities at the time of sale
- The seller would pay a franchise fee of $3,500 upon Subway approval
- The buyer would pay for the inventory at closing date— approximately $5,000
- The seller wanted all cash, no take back (Vendor take back financing)

Shayne's ongoing analysis included becoming familiar with how Subway managed its franchise community. He acquired a Subway franchise kit, which was very helpful. In addition to an initial franchise transfer fee of roughly $3500, the franchise would supply all the equipment and leaseholds, sign a premises sublease with Subway (they control all leases) and pay a weekly royalty fee of 8% of gross sales. In addition, a fee of 5% of gross sales was charged and remitted to SFAFT (Subway Franchise Advertising Fund Trust). This 5% would be spent on advertising the Subway brand nationally and locally. Fees to Subway and SFAFT were remitted weekly through pre-authorized payment.

During the analytical process, some questions needed to be answered. Could he run a restaurant? He and the rest of the family had no restaurant experience, and the possibility of running a fast-food operation seemed daunting. Shayne and my mother Beverly were able to work in three restaurants on different occasions before attending the University of Subway. U of S, located at Subway HQ in Milford, Connecticut, is where they took their official training before being anointed franchisees. During their two weeks at HQ, they spent forty hours at a Subway restaurant. They found the entire experience educational but highly stressful and nerve wracking. It was only after the first several months of running the store that Shayne became reasonably comfortable. But even after almost ten years, he was never stress-free.

The next question posed was, "What was Subway Corporate like?" Subway's chain of command starts with its president Fred De Luca and his partner Dr. Peter Buck. Dr. Buck bankrolled (lending $1,000) young De Luca when he was a teenager and suffice to say they are both quite wealthy today. By 2009, Subway had over 32,000 stores worldwide. In the past two decades, Entrepreneur magazine has voted the privately owned company the number one franchise (out of a list of five hundred) sixteen times. Without a doubt, it is the franchise of franchises. Throughout our tenure, our head office experience was a fair and satisfying one. The Milford operation is world class. Doctors Associates Inc. (the legal name and homage to Dr. Buck) assigns geographical locations to development agents who work on an independent commission basis. A portion of the 8% royalty fee remitted to Subway as a percentage of gross sales is earmarked for the local development agent (DA).

The geographical area known as ENO (Eastern and Northern Ontario) has as its largest cities Ottawa, Sudbury, Sault St. Marie,

Kingston, and our city, Peterborough. It is a vast geography, difficult to maintain, and poses a challenge for any DA wishing to grow the franchise base. Ken Fielding, with experience in the Dixie Lee fried chicken franchise industry, boldly took on the Subway DA challenge as the eighties ended. Starting with a single franchise in Peterborough, he grew his territory to over 230 stores by late 2009. He chose Minden, Ontario, as his head office because he lived there, and it was just about smack dab in the middle of his geographical territory. His staff was comprised of a general manager, two office employees, and six to eight field consultants who were the conduit between his office and franchisees. These consultants were, in most cases, the only tangible interface franchisees had. Ken Fielding or his general manager Mike Lopez would occasionally visit stores but relied on bi-annual meetings to preach the Subway gospel. These meetings took place at a central location, and it was mandatory that all franchisees attend, at their own expense.

THE PURCHASE

After gathering all information and an analysis that spanned several weeks, Shayne brought the idea to the family and came to the conclusion that the Subway experience suited us. As explained, most Subway transfers (resales) are executed with the seller taking a mortgage back from the buyer. In the case of Shayne's first purchase, the seller wanted cash. Shayne was able to scrounge up $60,000. Canadian banks loathe extending credit to restaurants and categorize them as poor credit risks. Because of his previous bankruptcy, Shayne had no luck with the banks. The shortfall was made up with a loan from a friend. Repayment to his associate would be over forty-eight months at 3% over the prime rate, secured by a promissory note.

Before he made an offer, Shayne familiarized himself with all of the key components associated with the current financial statements he received from the vendor, Dave Kjaer. Due diligence is a must when analyzing any potential franchise purchase.

His notes on his projected first year resembled the following:

INCOME STATEMENT (projected)

Sales	275,000	- 9% increase
Food Costs	(91,000)	- 33% (from 40%) no theft
Net	184,000	

Expenses		
Advertising and Promotion	15,000	- includes SFAFT
Bank Charges	1,200	- a credit union is cheaper
Insurance	700	- premises
Interest	1,800	- 40,000 @ 6.5%
Legal/Accounting	2,000	- Shayne does daily accounting
Office/Postage	1,500	
Rent	13,750	- incl. common maint. & taxes
Repairs and Maintenance	5,000	- equipment, snow plowing
Telephone/Internet	1,000	- one line only
Subway 8% Royalties	22,000	
Utilities	8,200	- gas and electric
Vehicle/Travel	800	- school lunch deliveries
Wages/Benefits	46,000	
Total	(114,450)	
Loan Repayment	(15,550)	- Promissory Note 40,000
Net Before Tax	50,000	

Bridgenorth Subway to the left of the Paulmac pet food store.

After making an offer to purchase, a meeting with the development agent, Ken Fielding Enterprises, ensued, followed by a large
amount of cumbersome paperwork. Subway HQ requires final
approval from the DA. When the buyer is approved, the final
stipulation is to complete the two-week training course in Milford,
CT, with a minimum grade of 80%.

His trip to Minden, Ontario (DA headquarters), an hour's drive
north of Peterborough, resulted in the much-anticipated meeting
with Ken Fielding. Fielding had started with Subway in 1989 and
initialized his first franchise in Peterborough. Since that time, as
the Subway name gained prestige, he grew his base of franchisees
dramatically. Ken Fielding Enterprises is now recognized by
Subway as one of the best development agent operations in North
America. By 2009, he had 230 restaurants under his supervision.
As we learned over time, his success was only exceeded by his
aloofness. An understated, moderately amiable exterior masked

a clever and calculating businessman. Fielding asked reasonable questions and expressed a confidence that theirs would be a rewarding and enjoyable relationship. Shayne left the interview with great elation, sensing a wonderful future ahead, and it would be, although not exactly as anticipated.

During the six-week period between the meeting with Fielding and the takeover of the store, Shayne continued to re-analyze income statement scenarios, confirm costs and future expenses, and visit and work in local Subway locations. He met with the Bridgenorth staff and looked at possible improvements to the future operation.

Shayne was able to analyze several of the WISRs (Weekly Inventory and Sales Reports) that the vendor had made available. The WISR is a document that is a product of the physical inventory you conduct at the end of a given week and the transactions you register in your POS (point of sale) machine through the week. The POS machine is the register for which you input each sale. It acts as a cash register and tracks every sale including the specific details of item sold. The data you input provides a delineated breakdown of food costs, sales, units sold, and expenses among other things. Each week the WISR is transmitted to headquarters via email, which enables Subway to extract their 8% royalty accurately from the franchisees bank account. The same is done for the 5% for SFAFT's (Subway Franchisee Advertising Fund Trust). Subway and SFAFT would consider the commission tally to be the main purpose of the WISR. Franchisees use it for a multitude of functions. Some are as follows:

- record sales (daily, weekly, monthly, and yearly)
- analyze average sales volumes
- record food and beverage costs and percentages of sales
- analyze average daily sales volumes
- compare each store to the ENO store average

- analyze each inventory item as a percentage of sales
- compare productivity (daily, weekly, monthly, and yearly)

The WISR is a tool that when interpreted properly can greatly improve your bottom line. By analyzing previous WISRs and after learning how to deconstruct a WISR properly at Subway school, Shayne saw immediately that, based on abnormal food cost figures, the unsupervised staff at the Subway in Bridgenorth must have been stealing food. If theft were eliminated, food costs would drop instantly.

He further deduced that an illuminated sign needed to be built near the road. The restaurant was set back about sixty feet from the curb, and at any rate of speed, a passing driver would not have much time to look inward and spot the store. However, a neon sign near the curb would be noticed at a simple glance and would be spotted from a distance if constructed at a height of twenty feet. A large, well-lit sign would cost at least $10,000, 10% of the cost of the franchise. It would turn out to be the best investment Shayne made at that location.

MEETING THE MAN

In April of 2000, Shayne anxiously awaited the takeover of his Subway restaurant. Short-term expectations included an increase in sales, a decrease in food and labour costs, which would result in a handsome bottom line. Our three to five year plan was to increase sales to $400,000 annually (a rise of 60%), decrease food costs to 33% of sales (down from 40%), and decrease labour costs to 18% (down from 34%).

At this time, my brother Kent and I waited as our old man got his affairs in order and completed the transaction. As teenagers more concerned with our social lives, playing sports, and causing trouble, the prospect of a part-time job was never overly exciting. However, it would put cash in our otherwise empty pockets and teach us all about work ethic and responsibility. My dad was the most excited, envisioning a positive experience for the whole family. My brothers and I simply saw it as a job where, as teenagers, we would be forced to spend more time with our parents. We would start as employees, technically the equals to an experienced yet undisciplined staff pensively awaiting their new boss.

Our exit strategy was a projected sale of the business at a minimum of twice the original purchase price of $100,000. The setting of both short and long term goals is important to ensure a successful venture. It's a business, not a love affair. Profit is the driving motive.

The heavy lifting began when Shayne and Beverly drove all the way to Milford, Connecticut, to undertake Subway training. The two-week sojourn included classroom training, interaction with about 150 prospective franchisees, a weeklong in-store immersion, and concluded with a four-hour examination requiring a passing grade of 80%.

After thirty-five years of marketing experience that included countless training courses and seminars, Shayne figured there wasn't much he hadn't seen. The in-store portion of the training was much anticipated, as this was virgin territory.

Early on, the assembled trainees were treated to an interaction with the incomparable Fred De Luca, Subway's founder. He told of his ascendance to franchising glory to a breathless crowd who hung on his every word. His journey truly captured the essence of the "American Dream." He explained that as a first-year college student looking for summer employment, he started a modest sandwich shop, funded by his friend Peter Buck, who loaned him what seems now as a paltry $1,000 to start up. Naming his store Pete's Subs in the beginning, De Luca told of his many missteps early on, and he spun the tale in his hallmark folksy manner, full of self-deprecation and pride in his humble beginnings. In an hour, he revealed all the ups and downs of establishing a handful of stores over his first ten years. His benefactor was now Dr. Peter Buck, and the name Subway had emerged. Eventually their company would become Doctor's Associates Inc. (DAI) using the Subway name and logo at each individual location. Some stores failed, new ones surfaced, and somewhere young Fred discovered the key during those early years. It was franchising. The rest is history. His methods of franchising and food management practices have become a world standard.

De Luca is a formidable hands-on businessman of the highest caliber. A polished veteran of the fast-food industry, he is a standard setter who is accessible, perceptive, and driven to be the best. And with his leadership, he has catapulted Subway to the top of the industry.

As De Luca effortlessly fielded questions that afternoon, Shayne wondered if any of Fred's contemporaries in the franchise industry were as accessible to each of their franchise partners. Later that week, while Shayne and Beverly were eating lunch in the cafeteria with their fellow Subway classmates, Fred sat down across from Shayne and asked him what kind of season the Peterborough Petes hockey team was having. McDonald's founder Ray Kroc probably didn't know where Peterborough was, even though there were four McDonald's in our small town. In earlier times, Shayne was an Apple computer dealer when Steve Jobs was a name without a face. Here in Milford was a leader with insight, passion, and purpose. Their interaction was the highlight of Shayne's decade with the company.

The University of Subway fortnight was draining yet enlightening. Shayne and Beverly found the classroom portions interesting and well paced with their various instructors but accompanied by exhaustive homework assignments—tough work for a middle-aged couple that hadn't been in school in over thirty years. The in-class portion combined with the forty-hour in-store foray left little time for them to catch their breath.

Passing the exam made the trip home a welcome relief. The experience served as the linchpin for an ensuing decade of success and left Shayne and Beverly with confidence and anticipation for the next stage of the process.

Shayne with Fred De Luca at Subway Training.

OUR NEW STORE

The most important lesson learned at Subway University is that the day-to-day operation of a Subway restaurant comes down to applying the practices learned during the training. In the end, it simply boils down to hard work. Being a marketing genius is irrelevant. The 5% royalty to SFAFT ensures the advertising of the brand, including national advertising. If it does its job, the ads will generate customers. Subway provides all the tools and planning necessary for success. There is an abundance of information and reports available to assist and measure your progress. If your location is correct, and you follow the lead, you will succeed.

The Subway training experience is so thorough that the daily running of the franchise has no surprises. Shayne knew the wild cards would be the employees and customers. A third wild card would later surface.

The purchase closed May 3, 2000. The transfer was a significant event in that it underlined how meticulous Subway is in its paperwork process. Documentation is totally weighed toward the franchisor. The myriad undertakings give zero wiggle room to the franchisee who is obliged to follow HQ's mandate. While there are many advantages to being a franchisee, you are locked into a regimen that is legally one-sided in favour of the franchisor. If you disobey the rules, the duration of your time as a franchisee will be limited. Over the years, Shayne would test the limits of Subway's tolerance.

The first day flashed by as we set into our new routine. We had inherited seven employees and with four family members also available, Shayne especially was excited about the challenge. At Sub School, it was emphasized that when franchises were transferred and employees were inherited there was usually a complete staff turnover during the first ninety days. During his due diligence period, he discovered that this staff was under supervised, and he was prepared for the inevitable exodus. Long ago Shayne had learned that "you should terminate employees at your own convenience, not theirs. However, it doesn't always turn out that way." Looming too, of course, was figuring out how to stop employees from continuing to steal food.

The strongest of the employees had been the manager under the previous owner, a seemingly bright young man who appeared to grasp the Subway mantra. He was the one most suited to help us become acclimated to our new store. Lo and behold, he threw in the towel in the midst of a busy shift on a holiday weekend, two weeks into our tenure. His parting words, "You'll get through it" became a phrase Shayne would repeat facetiously from that day forward. This employee's single act of cowardice displayed the worst side of employee behaviour. It became a great lesson as Shayne and Beverly, his two co-workers that day, did in fact "get through it" as we always did in similar circumstances in the future. But it wasn't easy, as you can imagine.

We also became acquainted with a slew of characters that frequented our store. Owning a restaurant that serves breakfast means that, inevitably, you will be providing a hangout for locals who will buy a ninety-nine cent coffee, read a free paper, use the washroom, and socialize with the staff while they work. In Bridgenorth, we had a world-class goldbricker that went by the name of Ian, who would come in with his girlfriend—it was a miracle he had one—buy a small coffee, refill it three times for free, read the free newspaper, use the washroom for ten minutes, complain that the washroom floor was dirty, then ask to borrow ten tomato boxes to help in his move. It seemed like he was moving every three months. He sold birdbaths out of a crumbling Ford Econoline van for a living and squatted in his late father's house. Before his father's death, Ian had been leeching money out of him from his severance checks. There will be many characters like Ian who want to hang out at your establishment, some more enjoyable than others.

As a franchisee in the quick-serve industry, you are always on call. Employee absences, running out of food items, unexpected customer disturbances and complaints, and maintenance issues are all predicaments employees are reluctant to act on. They would rather phone the owner and let him or her face the problem. Minimum wage has a way of excusing employees from assuming responsibility. There were, however, a few occasions where our best employees took charge.

A good example was when our freezer broke down one afternoon, and repairs would not be available until the next day. Angie Verheem, one of our best workers, South African by birth, was on duty. Enduring the brutally cold Canadian winters wasn't something she particularly embraced. On a -10 C day in February, she took advantage of the Canadian winter when she and another employee moved the entire contents of the freezer (about $5,000 in food) outside the building. She even borrowed a tarpaulin from a neighboring business so that the boxes of food were not visible to the public. That was a rare occasion when an employee decided to lead rather than follow.

The scheduling of staff hours is critical, as the nature of the quick-serve restaurant is contingent on customer flow and demand. If staff are sick or quit, family must pick up the slack, as there are no temps in this game. No one is ready to come off the bench. Randomly, some weeks can quickly become an eighty-hour grind.

We once hired a highly regarded applicant who had been recommended by an out-of-town franchisee. We promptly assigned him a full shift, knowing he was fully trained and would easily fit into our environment. The day he was to start, we received a call from his roommate telling us that he was quitting. Guess who covered the shift? This kind of stuff is part of the territory.

In the early days, we learned that minimum-wage employees would not only fail to make decisions on their own, they would panic. Be close to your phone. They will run out of patience immediately, won't attempt to fix an equipment malfunction, and will flip out if customers react negatively. Employees, like Angie, who are capable of making decisions on their own, are rare. When you find one, cultivate, nurture, and keep them financially motivated. Giving an employee a title (i.e., shift supervisor), bolsters their self-esteem and honours a strong work ethic.

*Shayne and Beverly Randall behind the counter
of the Bridgenorth store.*

HUNTING AND GRUNTING

There are a few areas outside of the Subway blueprint that franchisees can explore to increase sales. As it was earlier related, a large, illuminated sign was installed early on in Bridgenorth. We immediately were rewarded with an 8% increase in business. The sign had such an impact that many first-time customers commented that they were unaware that there was a Subway restaurant in Bridgenorth. The store was six years old at that point, and these people had been driving by almost every day.

We also rented a portable sign that we placed near the road. It usually had a simple message that we changed every month, or we would use it to advertise help wanted. Shayne describes this early part of the evolution as, "Hunting and Grunting." During the initial six months he prepared and delivered complimentary sandwich platters to every business within two kilometers, one at a time, three days a week, usually days when sales were lower so that extra staff wasn't required. He continued to expand the reach so that on completion he had "plattered" all businesses within ten kilometers. He left coupons with every delivery and tracked them to see if the employees of these businesses were actually coming to our store, which they did.

Shayne visited every school in the county, offering a discounted lunch program. In our third year, we had fourteen schools in our lunch program. Each school was provided lunch once a month. He would come in at midnight, bake bread, and make the lunches. This incremental business "was like finding money on the street" he would say. It was astounding that other franchisees were not tapping the school lunch market. These kids were our future customers. We promoted a healthy diet as many of the students frequented our stores right into adulthood. It is a small community after all.

Street sign for the Bridgenorth store.

GETTING OUR GROOVE

Early in our tenure, monitoring customer tendencies and evaluating staff became critical items. In May of 2000, when we took over the Bridgenorth operation, it was coming into its busiest time of the year, so we had to make adjustments on the fly. We made extra bread, ordered extra food from our supplier, and had plenty of staff on duty at appropriate times. Customers were quick to notice. They weren't waiting in line as long, and everything on the menu was always available. Back in 2000, we served either white or wheat bread, and there was only one type of cheese. This is a far cry from the large variety offered today.

We were getting accustomed to the characters we interacted with. This was a customer service industry, and we had to develop our skills and reputation as customer servers, which meant dealing with low and high maintenance patrons alike. There was a short haggard man who would come in and ask to feel the bread to verify its freshness. We always declined the request, but he continued to ask with every visit. One day he had come to a conclusion. "I was gonna rob you guys, but I don't think I will now. You guys run a good place. You take care of your customers." He thoroughly enjoyed flashing a fake thousand-dollar bill he had when it was time to pay. "Can I pay with this baby? Ha-ha, I'm only kidding." After ringing his sub in, he would ask in a perfunctory tone, "Can I get some extra stamps? It's for the kids; I do it through the Home Depot." "Sorry sir, we don't do that." "Yes, you do, I do it all the time. It's for the kids." He'd try that scam every visit.

(Subway used to have a rewards system where customers were given stamps when they purchased subs that they would then collect and eventually reimburse for a free sub. The program was abolished after a large amount of counterfeiting was discovered. It escalated to where rolls of stamps were being sold on Ebay. It has since been replaced by a points card, which has proven to be an invaluable promotion.)

By the end of our first summer, we had reached a competence level as an operation. We had fired and hired, trained and retrained, and were noticing improvements in sales. Our field consultant (FC), Steve Green, was informative and helpful, available when needed and his monthly evaluations revealed our shortcomings and the areas that needed improvement. The dialogue was open and consistent, and while we were apprehensive before he arrived to perform his inspections, he marked our store fairly. Subway sets a high standard, and while franchisees didn't look forward to the FC's monthly visits, they knew it is a vital component in continuing the success of the brand.

Steve Green was our first FC, and as we were struggling with just running the restaurant, we weren't exactly sure how he would interact with us. He was gregarious and informative but when tested with questions did not always have an immediate answer. He was certainly familiar with all Subway regulations and made sure we had a thorough understanding of them. But when Shayne asked him to assist in locating a supplier for a neon roadside sign we wanted to install, Green had no idea whom to recommend. Our Subway HQ coordinator, Barb McMellon, was very helpful in guiding Shayne in the right direction.

During our first year, a nearby franchisee experienced a bacterial problem via a sick employee that manifested itself in a flu outbreak after a school lunch was provided. Throughout our decade, this was the lone incident of food poisoning we were aware of. It was an affirmation of the importance Subway placed on hand-washing and glove usage. One errant employee's negligence could lead to a business-destroying experience.

All restaurants in Ontario, as is surely the case in most jurisdictions, are subject to the scrutiny of the local department of public health. Our stores were inspected quarterly by the Public Health Department and subject to many of the criteria that our FC used when he performed his monthly Subway evaluation. In our ten-year experience, we never experienced a single public health violation or complaint. There is no doubt that the Subway ENO evaluations involved a far deeper analysis and a higher standard. Subway set the bar high, which undoubtedly contributed to the enjoyed successes, but did put a high degree of stress on the franchisees and their staff as they scrambled to meet the requirements. Most franchisors in the restaurant industry do not have such a frequent and thorough internal evaluation process.

Steve Green was cordial and businesslike, reflecting the positive rapport we enjoyed with ENO that first year. Ken Fielding hosted a Christmas party for our district, showing a longed-for jovial side that we never saw again. In late January of 2001, Green invited Shayne to a Super Bowl party sponsored by Pepsi, our beverage supplier. Sales were up 15%, we had reduced food and labour costs, and customer complaints were non-existent to our knowledge. We were in a groove. ENO had about a hundred stores then, and any franchisee that overachieved was acknowledged. At that stage in his career, Fielding seemed to appreciate his franchisee's efforts.

In February 2001, an event occurred that would have a latent effect on our relationship with ENO. Many moons ago, Shayne, as a photocopier franchisee, engaged in informal meetings with fellow dealers that were of great benefit. He was encouraged to organize such a meeting with about a dozen Subway owners who had stores in the immediate area. The purpose was to discuss common problems and opportunities. It didn't occur to him to ask

ENO to join the meeting or to get their approval for such a gathering. Call it naïveté, but he never thought they would consider this taboo.

Shayne received a phone call from Green shortly after the meeting took place, informing him that this sort of meeting was not condoned. Interestingly enough, Shayne had previously informed Green of the meeting before it occurred, and there was no argument at that time. Shayne explained his position and added that the meeting hadn't been fruitful and that he wasn't aware that it was a no-no. Shayne assured Green that he wouldn't convene any more meetings in the future. Although Green seemed content with Shayne's guarantee, the relationship with ENO wasn't quite the same thereafter. The mandate from Ken Fielding seemed to be to receive as little input from his franchisees as possible.

FAMILY

Our first year was nearing conclusion with increased sales and excellent profits. By spring 2001, we noticed some franchisees were selling their stores. This was an evergreen occurrence and is part of a healthy franchise system. After all, everyone should have an exit target and with sales/resales occurring, it certainly was a good sign for the Subway brand. A newly developed store cost around $200,000 at that time, while buying an existing franchise cost about 50% of its annual sales. Shayne had paid 40% of Bridgenorth Subway's annual sales in May of 2000, and it felt like a bargain.

He had become a member of the SFAFT board, which made him privy to the Subway hierarchy and allowed him to convene with four different boards under the Subway umbrella. Franchisees at that time were a mix of gender, ethnic origins, and age. Eager, energetic, bright, and hard working, these were hands-on operators. The majority of them were born in Canada. I mention this because that paradigm would shift dramatically in the years to come. We discovered that the economic promise Canada offered was taken for granted by some of its citizens but was embraced with vigour by new friends from afar. Their enthusiasm and energy would elevate them to a prominent position in the Subway franchise family and effectively discourage others from trying to compete with their dogged determination and the low labour costs that their family involvement afforded.

While he was a member of the SFAFT board, many franchisees

would seek Shayne's advice. He would field numerous queries from them and as more Indian franchisees came into the fold, they relied on him as their spokesman. Shayne and I admired both their courage in adopting a new country and in learning a new language. Their work ethic and family dynamic reminded him of a disappearing Canadian way of life. Times were changing.

What sustained our business throughout these times was the presence of family. We were all-Subway all day. We talked Subway around the dinner table, around the television, on days off, all the time. It was on our minds because it was a big part of our lives, especially for my old man. We had nicknames for customers, employees, and all the working members of the family. We pushed each other, ragged on one another, and celebrated all successes no matter how trivial, especially Shayne, an accomplished self-promoter (which I say as a compliment) who saw this as an adventure, with a beginning and an end. Make no mistake, he thirsted for success, but we all knew we were just making sandwiches. We weren't saving lives. Shayne's kids, still in school, saw Subway as a means to an end while Shayne's life work had already come and gone. The end of his business career was coming soon.

The Subway pipeline from India was just in its infancy, but the newcomers would mark the beginning of an impregnable surge that would solidify Subway as the #1 franchise in the world and ensure it stayed there for a long time. But for Canadians hoping to be future franchisees, the train was quickly leaving the station.

I was nineteen and enrolled at a local university to study Business and English Literature. Trent University was a ten-minute drive away. My brothers Kent and Nolan were in high school. We were all eager to earn some extra money, even if it meant working with our parents. Shayne and Beverly saw it as a great way to interact with their kids while giving them an alternative to idle time and mischief. We grew up a little, learned some people skills, and it taught me a new type of work ethic. Shayne was dependant on the five of us being the labour nucleus of the business. We knew that premise had a time limit. Back in the spring of 2001, however, we had an interlude of success and great expectation.

CANCER

On May 4, 2001, one year and one day after we acquired our first Subway store, my dad was diagnosed with prostate cancer. With impending surgery, roles and responsibilities had to be altered. Shayne looked at it as an opportunity to overcome an obstacle.

My youngest brother Darcy, then 12, had congenital glaucoma and was successfully operated on at Sick Kids Hospital in Toronto at six months of age. The glaucoma became a minor inconvenience when compared to his subsequent diagnosis of autism as a two-year-old. Non-verbal until the age of seven, our family and network were continually striving to improve his life. Compared to the 24/7 stress of caring for Darcy, prostate cancer neither intimidated nor discouraged my parents or the rest of us.

After his recovery, Shayne would and still does brag about the amount of cancers (he also had basal cell carcinoma) and physical ailments he's conquered as if they were red badges of courage. Having said that, it was a tough time, and we endured with heavy hearts. Looking back, Shayne describes this as a "watershed moment that tested our mettle and conditioned us for the battles to come."

Being the pugnacious character that he is, Shayne decided to postpone his prostate surgery into late October, some six months distant. Despite protests from the family and friends, he had decided that he couldn't miss any of the summer months when business was booming in "cottage country." As it turned out, he was really pushing the envelope. When they removed the tumour in late October, it was discovered he had been carrying it for about ten years. He hadn't earned the nickname "lucky bastard" in error. Years later, he cheated death once again when a city bus t-boned his vehicle after the bus ran a red light. The car was demolished, and he escaped with merely a banged-up hand, another red badge of courage.

In spite of the impending surgery, adjustments were made that summer and fall, and we all thrived through his illness and recuperation. The rest of the family spread the load around while the store continued to operate smoothly. Sales were good, and profits met our expectations.

Shayne hired a third-year Trent student, Eric Ingram, who had worked at one of ENO's most heralded stores in the small town of Lakefield, a ten-minute drive away. ENO used the Lakefield store for franchisee training, and the store's franchisee was considered a darling among the ENO crew. The husband of this franchisee was abusive to Ingram and some of the rest of the staff. Eric, put off by the conduct of the husband, had had enough and dropped off a resume at our shop. When he joined us, he immediately became our most efficient worker and sort of acted as a sandwich artist mentor for my brothers and me as we picked up the slack in Shayne's absence. He improved our ability as workers and helped propel the operation to new heights. Although he and Shayne butted heads a little bit, only natural for two such characters, Eric would say his experience working for us redeemed his opinion of Subway, something he didn't think was possible after his time at the store in Lakefield.

KEN FIELDING

Shayne attended the semi-annual ENO operations meeting that fall, and it was then that he got a better insight into how Ken Fielding Enterprises (ENO) operated. About 120 franchisees assembled at the Deerhurst Resort in Huntsville, Ontario, in the beautiful Muskoka district.

The second day of the two-day event had suppliers stage a late afternoon trade show followed by food and drinks. This was much more useful than the proceedings of day one. The first day began with an introduction from Ken Fielding. Fielding—picture a Caucasian Buddha in plainclothes—spoke to his audience in a steadily quiet way and voiced his opinions of SFAFT, the politics of Subway, and any general topics he felt were pertinent. Many would interpret his public speaking as condescending and detached. His lack of one-on-one interaction with the attendant franchisees and his short participation in the meeting was surprising to Shayne. After his brief message, he left the rest of the meeting to Mike Lopez, his general manager, and his field consultants to cover while he hovered around the proceedings.

Lopez would take over the proceedings in a slightly more congenial manner. But he was an extension of his mentor Fielding and would continue the tone set early on by his boss. Shayne thirsted to learn new ideas and methods, new products and opportunities. He wanted to strengthen our relationship with our DA, as it would surely help us in the long haul.

Shayne got to fraternize with other franchisees at the meeting.

Most were unanimous in their opinion of Fielding. It wasn't positive.

As the Subway brand escalated in importance among competitors in the quick-serve industry, Fielding had also achieved great success. It seemed that with this success, Subway HQ had developed a sterner and less amiable relationship with its DAs. In turn, the DAs echoed that position when interacting with franchisees. Even though as franchisees we wanted a friendlier rapport with our DA, the relationship dynamic between DA and franchisee was changing.

Dylan behind the counter of the Bridgenorth store serving his grandfather, Fenwick Randall.

KEY PARTNERSHIPS

Important to the success of a franchise is the establishment of meaningful alliances with an accountant and a lawyer. Missing from the list you might think is a banker. Banks are not fond of the restaurant segment and with justification. Two-thirds of restaurant start-ups do not survive twenty-four months. You should depend on the vendor or other sources to help finance a franchise purchase. You will not change the stance of the banks so don't waste your time. The instruments banks like to use as collateral are not always prevalent in a Subway franchise. There are no receivables, assets depreciate rapidly, and goodwill is only frowned upon. Shayne wasn't able to arrange a vendor take-back (mortgage) with his first Subway acquisition, but as resale prices escalated over the years, vendors would almost always take back part of the purchase in the form of a promissory note or a mortgage.

He was able to secure an excellent lawyer right from the start who had good experience with buying and selling Subways. This partnership became invaluable over the years and saved considerable time and stress. He kept the same accounting firm he had had for the previous thirty years, which meant another hurdle was avoided. The legal and accounting areas are two of the most important partnerships in the success of a franchise of any kind. Another plus was Shayne's ability to do his own in-house accounting. This kept fees low and gave him an ongoing awareness of the daily fluctuations of the store. He performed banking functions, prepared payroll, and remitted all payments to suppliers and government agencies. He took great pride in having monthly profit and loss statements ready by the second of the month. Online banking made reconciliations quick and easy. At age sixty, he upped his computer IQ, saving him time, money, and aggravation. He calculated that over the years he saved about $15,000 in bank fees by using a credit union in lieu of a bank. Shop around. All banks aren't created equal.

Our biggest expense was the cost of food. As a percentage of sales, it fluctuated between 28% and 38% over the years. Sound attention to this expense is vital to the success of the business because in addition to labour, it is an unfixed cost. The WISR tracks each food item as a percentage of sales. Fluctuations in these percentages indicate a problem. Not charging for extra items such as cheese or bacon, not ringing in a friend's sandwich, or staff leaving the store with a package of steak in their backpack are situations that can occur. It also helps to curry a good relationship with your food suppliers. Our bills were always paid promptly (by internet) and delivery people were always rewarded with a cool drink. We had a great relationship with Sysco, from the people we met from corporate positions to the drivers who were prompt and reliable with their deliveries. Any errors made by either party—us or Sysco—with regards to food orders were quickly corrected without any disputes. Sysco treated their customers very well and as such became the standard to which all suppliers were measured.

You also have a partnership with employees that must be nurtured constantly. Congratulations were always offered and criticism always administered in a private setting. With a few exceptions, employees were always protected when customers complained. By accepting and deflecting the blame as a manager, customers can be diffused and calmed and employees given the benefit of the doubt. Staff morale and loyalty will increase.

Shayne or I would always ask employees to immediately report a customer complaint directly to one of us. Employees like the fact that they do not have to directly act on the complaint. Customers appreciate when their complaints are acknowledged and the manager becomes involved in making an assessment.

Surprisingly, we received a few complaints in regard to customers cracking or breaking a tooth while eating a sandwich. Although tooth damage may have occurred, it was never attributed to food preparation. After a few wild goose chases, it was ascertained that people would go to great lengths to try and get someone else to pay for their dental work.

Subway Franchisee Advertising Fund Trust (SFAFT) is the entity that decides how every advertising dollar is spent. It is administered by franchisees and staffed by paid employees who are supposedly controlled by the SFAFT board of directors. Shayne had the confidence of most of the franchisees and was encouraged to be a director, a title he held for most his time with Subway. The franchisees nominated him to be president at one point even though he was absent from that particular meeting. Shayne never turned a fellow franchisee down but deferred on this occasion as we were in the process of selling our final store. I have a feeling Fielding was surprised when they nominated Shayne for SFAFT president.

Subway headquarters was and still is a remarkable organization. Always available and informative, the head office is the culmination of decades of improvisation and refined technique. They were our best partnership and enabled us to achieve success. There was always a coordinator at Subway HQ to answer questions.

As time would tell, our partnership with our development agent Ken Fielding (who represented ENO), would prove to be the weakest of all. Unique to us, we had the feeling that our DA and his organization were discouraging rather than encouraging.

HIRING AND FIRING

Deciding whom to hire is the most important task you will be confronted with. Without a competent staff, it doesn't matter how you perform in all other facets of the business. Your store will collapse like a house of cards, especially if it is a high-volume operation where the potential for disaster is greater. You trust these people with serving, baking, making subs, cleaning, and handling money. You can't rely on just anyone, which makes family a valuable asset. By and large, family members won't steal, gossip, concoct phony excuses for absences, and can be relied on to perform all tasks on their own without supervision.

We had success hiring university students because of their intelligence and desperate need for money, even if it came from a minimum wage job. Many stores hire older women in their forties as managers which does work in many instances, and I have witnessed many that fit well at their respective stores. We had more success with people in their twenties. At Chemong Road in 2004, we made one of our best moves when we hired Michelle Scott, a stalwart who never missed an open Monday to Friday and who continues to work there now. She was always rewarded for her honesty, loyalty, and highly efficient work. After six years, she had her morning shift down to a science. Invaluable as a baker, trainer, and sandwich artist, she was as close to irreplaceable as an employee can be and was compensated accordingly. Like a diamond in the rough, you treasure this type of employee.

However, we have found these people hard to find. Some

managers prefer to hire females because they are known as better multitaskers or because the franchisee is female and women are just more comfortable interacting with women. If any labor board knew of this practice, they might cry discrimination but the bottom line is to hire people who are qualified, that you are comfortable with, and that you trust. We preferred university students, not to be confused with high school kids who we generally deemed too immature and uncommitted. As sandwich artists, these older students could relate and interact socially with the clientele.

When in need of new workers at the final store we purchased in 2007, located in a busy student housing area, we would often put a message on our street sign. The resumes would come flooding in. The sheer number of resumes warranted a screening process where I would instruct my most trusted employee working during the hours I wasn't there to accept the resumes and ask a very quick series of questions:

- Are you looking for part time or full time?
- Are you a student?
- Where do you live?
- Have you worked at a Subway or any other fast food chain before?
- What was your last job?
- What have you been doing since your last job?

As the employee is asking the questions, I would tell him or her to try to get an impression of what kind of person they were talking to. This is a pretty subjective task for an employee. Therefore, their perception of the applicant would be taken at face value.

Once I had established who the good applicants were, I would call them in for an interview. In the interview, I would try to intimidate them by telling them how tough the job was and that we have absolutely no patience for stealing or lateness and that we catch thieves quicker than the police does. We wanted to set a tone from the onset. I would tell them that Shayne was so proficient at catching thieves that he turned it into a game. He seemed to almost delight in catching the culprit and consequently scaring the life out of the individual. He never called the police. I think he thought his scare tactics might help reform them.

His practice stopped abruptly after catching someone who was the last person one would suspect as a thief. Adam was a fresh-faced, red haired, innocent-looking kid whose father was a school principal. Liked by our family and staff, Shayne had a particularly difficult time confronting him, forcing him to admit his crimes, and subsequently firing him. Although Shayne threatened to call the police and Adam's parents, he never followed through on the threats. He was convinced that the confrontation would put Adam back "on the straight and narrow."

Adam would commit suicide six months later. Shayne and the rest of us were devastated at the news, Shayne in particular, thinking that he might have contributed to Adam's decision, even though the kid's problems were much deeper than petty thievery. Shayne never played the intervention card again.

After warning applicants about the consequences of stealing, we would ask them questions about their previous employment and try to ascertain why they were not working with these organizations anymore. If the person said he or she was unhappy with the way the company was operating, I would be skeptical. Either party could have been at fault. It could be a 50% chance the employee was in the wrong and just had an arrogant attitude towards his or her previous employer. If the applicant had Subway experience, I would ask what store they worked for and call the store for a reference. When I called the store, I would ask one simple question: Would you hire this person again? If there was hesitation, we didn't hire that applicant.

Once you have made the decision to hire someone—you like

the resume, think the person is intelligent, will get along with your current staff, and will be reliable—you still never know what you are truly getting. This makes the training process that much more important. If you've hired a bad employee and don't know it yet, the best thing to do is have that person exposed as quickly as possible through a fair yet strenuous training process. The good employees will find it fair while the bad ones will think it is strenuous.

A great training tool that has in recent years become a compliance issue, and rightfully so, is the completion of Subway University courses, an online-training source that covers just about all the conceivable elements of working in a Subway restaurant. The courses are quick, simple, and allow employees to reaffirm what they already know and become educated in areas that are unclear. Each employee is given a password that only the franchisee and the employee can access, which makes cheating next to impossible.

We would insist that a new employee take fourteen Subway University courses online, which we paid them to complete, to help them become acclimated before they even put on a uniform. If they didn't complete the courses, they weren't hired. Their first shift would be during a busy period where ringing the sale through the cash register would be their first task. Throw them on the line and see what they can do on the till. Monitor their progress: Are they getting faster? Are they up-selling? Are they friendly? Relaxed yet efficient? Can they make a sub? Are they eagerly looking for work to do when the line dies down and there are no more subs to ring in? The last question is key. If they are looking for work and not standing around, it usually means they will have a good work ethic. In the ensuing shifts, monitor whether the trainee is performing tasks on their own without asking questions more than once, and you will quickly discover if they have an ability to be a multitasker. Are they making the subs quickly, neatly, and to formula? It only takes one or two shifts, with the proper monitoring, to get a grasp for what kind of talent you have. If you know the person is not going to make it, cut ties as quickly as possible.

When comprising your workforce, you have to formulate what kinds of shifts you are going to have and how many full-time versus part-time employees you want. In your franchisee training at Milford, they will instruct you on scheduling, but it will take some experience for you to truly understand how to use your staff most effectively based on the type of workforce available to you.

"Productivity," in Subway jargon, is a term for quantifying how efficiently your staff works based on the sandwich-unit sales the store makes during that employee's shift. The goal is to attain a productivity of between eight and twelve, meaning that for every hour worked by an employee, eight to twelve subs should be sold. This factors into all the work an employee does in an hour such as: food preparation, cleaning, dishwashing, cleaning the customer area, baking and storing bread, and stocking the sandwich unit. The employee needs to be able to do it all. This is where scheduling becomes very demanding because you are constantly aiming for this goal of eight to twelve.

Imagine your store's productivity was at eight. Most likely staff morale would be very high because they aren't being pushed to work hard. When attempting to improve productivity you should suggest that employees enhance their effort, which doesn't always sit well with them. You have to constantly encourage and motivate them. If we ever had a busy lunch, I would always brag to the other employees about the amount of units we did in an hour. Try and create an environment where the employees can take pride in their work. Praise them when they have a productive hour. Then suddenly the attitude changes from, "We are being worked too hard" to "I am a sub-making machine, and this shift just flew by."

Certain employees want it to be busy so they don't get bored.

Others try to get away with giving as little effort as they can. You need to facilitate a culture with workers who are there to work hard the whole shift. At this point, you will see your productivity numbers go up. Customer lineups will be minimal, and workers won't have to stay past their allotted time. Increased productivity results in increased profit. When productivity goes up, reward employees with raises.

There are two other ways to raise productivity. Cut back on hours, which is something no one wants to do but is necessary if sales are diminishing. The other, a more glamourous alternative, is to increase business. Again, it is all an attitude with your workers. When sales go up, do they rise to the occasion and continue to work hard, or do they get frustrated that they have to do more work? You have to promote an atmosphere where hard work is second nature because as mindless as this work may appear to be, it can be very physically demanding. Not everyone is cut out for it.

Through our experience, we found that the best workers were students who were usually unavailable full time, except during the summers. This made it difficult to obtain a lot of full-time workers. It is much easier to run a store with all full-time workers because there is more consistency in their work habits on a day-to day basis. Furthermore, when employees are doing the same tasks over and over again, they get better at it and ultimately the productivity of the store goes up. One weakness at our final store, incidentally a twenty-four-hour a day operation, was that we had trouble finding and training good full-time people. It was easy acquiring and grooming part-time students, which resulted in those part-timers collectively working as a platoon. What we lacked in routine and consistency, we more than made up for with each individual's effectiveness. However, I would still prefer to have a store with more quality full-time people.

INHERITING STAFF

When taking over an existing restaurant you must come in realizing that all the current employees are going to resent you. They were comfortable with the old owners, and any deviations from their routine are threatening and irritating to them. They will assume you do not know what you are doing, even though you have taken the mandatory two-week training course and maybe even worked at a Subway before. It does not matter to them because even minimum-wage jobs are inundated with arrogant employees who believe in their superior knowledge of the business whether or not it is warranted. They think their way is better.

Now I know you are thinking that every Subway is run identically because it is franchise with myriad rules and standards that must be abided by. This is very true. However, how you run your store can vary in how you deal with your employees, how they are treated, the policies you impose on them, and many other factors. Something as seemingly minute as end-of-shift tasks can vary from store to store, and how employees interpret their responsibilities will greatly affect their respect for the boss and, ultimately, how they perform.

All three of the Subways we have owned have been existing stores, and thus we have encountered the difficulties of inheriting staff. The more stores we owned, the better we handled each new staff. Shayne and I are not people you are going to push over or manipulate. When confronted with those inevitably arrogant employees, one of us would end up arguing with them, and they would quit, or we would fire them. Eliminate the arrogance, or it will drive you crazy.

There is one thing you do not want at your Subway, which can be the most daunting problem for a franchisee. That is employee unrest put upon by a clever, yet pretentious employee who is upset with the way the store is being run. It only takes one employee, who is usually decently efficient, who thinks they could be in charge and do a better job than you do. They will make an impression on the other employees and try to start a mutiny. If this person successfully influences the other employees, you are going to have a problem. Eliminate these people before they destroy the morale at your store. Strive to find and train employees that believe in your way of doing things.

The most memorable upheaval occurred when Shayne bought the Chemong Road location in 2004. I was still managing the Bridgenorth store and therefore did not experience it firsthand. There were three girls working at Chemong when Shayne took over who thought of themselves as the best workers on staff. One was officially the manager. Under the previous owner, their work environment was similar to a lounge where smoke breaks were frequent, and the morning hours were overstaffed, so when Shayne entered the fray I knew there would be some resistance. When he took over, as is always the case with new ownership, a few changes were made. He informed the manager, and she agreed to institute a reasonable list of changes that, if she were able to employ successfully, would be reimbursed with a bonus on her paycheque. When payday arrived, she asked Shayne why she didn't receive her bonus. A ridiculous question to ask when she blatantly refused to implement any of the modest changes Shayne asked of her. She promptly quit, exiting alongside the other two girls who were unwilling to accommodate their boss's moderate requests. Employees don't want to work harder than they feel they have to, especially if a new person is asking them.

Shayne in front of the till at the Bridgnorth store.

PART II

BUMPS IN THE ROAD

Shayne, on the road to good health after successful cancer surgery in 2002, maintained the promise of continuing on the path to our lofty goals. Steve Green, our field consultant, rarely marked us out of compliance, and his evaluations reflected a well-run operation, up to Subway's lofty standards. Steve provided a good dialogue and would discuss and suggest improvements that could be made.

In April, Shayne was approached by three different parties inquiring to purchase the Bridgenorth store. It was a time to pause and reflect. Our relationship with Subway HQ was excellent. Sales had risen 15% each year, and profits were formidable, due to our decrease in food costs and increase in productivity. Back then, ENO tolerated us in spite of Shayne calling the ill-fated franchisee meeting the year before. We were running an efficient and profitable store, staff turnover was low, and most importantly customers loved the service and the product. We had become a welcome stop for patrons who shortly before had been driving by our store.

The only question was why would Shayne want to sell when things were going so well? After considering all of these factors, I still had a handle on how my old man's mind works. I knew he would probably want to sell at this point because he was getting bored and probably felt he had reached a ceiling in this particular venture. For him the journey was more important than the destination, and he had arrived at his targeted goals. It was either get out or reset and acquire more stores. His health was still suspect, the kids had varied agendas, and his sixtieth birthday was approaching.

On April 22, we received a solid offer complete with a sizeable deposit from a schoolteacher and her family. The offer met the first criteria. It was almost twice the original purchase price, and it comprised all cash upon closing. With some reluctance, the offer was accepted. I wasn't bothered by the news, as I knew it would be a good deal for Shayne, and I looked at Subway as a part-time job to help me get through university. On the other hand, my old man reflected that, "If the transfer was able to occur, what new adventure would the Randalls embark on next?"

The Subway transfer process usually takes eight to twelve weeks, which would mean the buyer's completion of Subway training would need to take place during the summer. This was critical as our buyer only had a two-month window to complete the training before her school teaching started in the fall. Her husband and family were expected to run the day-to-day operation while she continued to teach. The Subway application required that she, as the franchisee, be obligated to successfully complete the Subway University training. There were no exceptions. No training—no store.

The paperwork and interview process went smoothly. However, ENO was unable to arrange for the buyer to take the training course during her two-month summer window. Subway University is held every two weeks during the year except during July and August when it is offered every four weeks. The deal blew up when ENO was unable to exert its influence to include our buyer in enrollment for Subway training. Shayne was disappointed but not despondent. Business was very strong that summer, and our vigour was renewed by those results.

I knew at this point that Shayne would rethink the process and attempt to find new opportunities to expand.

EXPANSION

Numbers fascinated and motivated Shayne. His copious records were his scorecard. In our first two full years as neophyte restaurateurs, we had increased our annual sales to $350,000, a 40% increase from a store that had already existed for six years. We reduced our food costs from 39% to 30%, and our labour costs declined to 17% compared to a Subway guideline of 22%. Profitability too was extraordinary. ENO however didn't seem that impressed. Our FC's evaluations focused on compliance items, and profit was not on that list. They gave lip service to profitability over the years and not once in a decade did they or anyone from Subway ask to see our financial statements. Wasn't profit the reason behind entering this venture?

After the schoolteacher's deal fell through, we regrouped and actually began looking at adding another Subway location to the family's holdings. At the Bridgenorth store, we had trained a very good staff, five family members were guarding the coffers, and the Subway brand was surging. This may be surprising, but I had an inkling that Shayne was getting too comfortable, almost bored with running the store as it had become easy for us to operate. Either he would buy another store to spice things up and present a new challenge, or he would sell and pursue a new project.

Late in the fall of 2002, we approached our closest fellow franchisees, Tom and Linda Cook, about acquiring their store located on Chemong Road, which was within walking distance of our residence. They were both around Shayne's age, ran a great store, and after his dogged pestering they seemed to warm to the idea. Their sales were about $425,000 annually. Their location at the north end of Peterborough on Chemong Road was due to be upgraded to the new Tuscany décor, at an estimated cost of about $60,000. Using the same principles we used to buy our first Subway franchise, we determined that all criterions could be met. We offered $175,000, with a vendor take-back of $50,000. Calculating the upgrade of $60,000, we would be investing $235,000 in the venture or 55% of annual sales. At this point, the Indian surge had started, but Peterborough had not yet felt its impact, hence the purchase price percentage of sales hadn't escalated as much as in other regions. Ratios of 60-70% of sales had been reported in larger areas like Toronto and Ottawa, but good value still existed in our neck of the woods.

Linda and Tom had purchased this store in 1999 after Linda had managed it for David Kjaer, the man who sold us our original store in Bridgenorth. Linda, having spent many years in the restaurant business in Toronto, had moved with Tom to Buckhorn, just north of Peterborough and lived right on the lake. It was an ideal spot for them to settle down after retirement. The Cooks had grown tired of dealing with ENO, and this appeared to be a good opportunity for them to part ways.

THE GREEN INCIDENT

As the Cooks pondered our offer, another event took place. Suzanne Green, wife of our field consultant Steve Green, was well along in establishing a new Subway location in Peterborough's largest shopping mall. This new location was to be situated a stone's throw from an existing Subway operated by Flo Card, a longtime franchisee. The proposed proximity of the two stores was puzzling but not as bizarre as the other circumstances connected to the venture. Many franchisors in the QSR industry do not assign restricted territories but have a very detailed protocol when agreeing to establish a new location. Besides traffic surveys, customer questionnaires, and population densities, the closest franchisee to the newly proposed site must be consulted. If it is determined that the closest franchisee's business will suffer, the project could be stopped. All other area franchisees are notified and can object if they feel that an additional location will hinder their present or future sales.

In the case of Suzanne Green's venture, it was fait accompli without Subway/ENO notifying the appropriate parties. A lease had been signed, and the project well was along before the news finally leaked. As Shayne was a SFAFT director at the time, he received two or three irate franchisee calls. All were adamant that this was not only unfair, but also unethical, as this new franchisee was the wife of an ENO employee. This was an ENO employee, who inspected their stores and could impact the present and future value of their franchises. He could conceivably subjectively mark them out of compliance to favour his wife's store, thereby decreasing the value of other franchises.

Although Shayne had assured Green that he would not convene any more meetings, this was a compelling reason to break that promise. Flo Card and Linda Cook were old pals as well, having worked for Dave Kjaer together in the past, and Shayne's first call concerning this mess came from Linda who was quite vocal in defense of her friend Flo. She also was not a fan of Steve Green whom was always the butt of her and Flo's jokes. Shayne felt compelled to act, and the fact we were trying to purchase Linda's store was an added reason to investigate the matter further.

They convened January 16, 2003 and offered an invitation to Steve Green who attended while his wife was not invited. Steve Green assured all present that the protocols were followed and that he would be fair in his future evaluation visits. Eventually however, new field consultants were appointed to our area, and Green was shuffled elsewhere in the organization.

The episode bothered Ken Fielding and from then on fortified Shayne's role as a rebel in Ken's eyes. Coincidentally, Suzanne Green did not attend that meeting but did initialize her store in the mall shortly thereafter. Less than three years later, she, along with Flo Card and Linda Cook, had vanished from the Subway landscape as a new type of franchisee was populating the Kawartha territory.

BOOKING THE COOKS

Shayne presented an offer to the Cooks, and it was accepted on February 6, 2003, about three weeks after the meeting about Suzanne Greene's opening of her store. The Cooks, after witnessing ENO stonewall our attempts to provide her friend Flo with a bit of justice, were now convinced that they wanted to end their association. By the time Shayne met with ENO in Minden to arrange the transfer, it was the end of April. Mike Lopez had assumed many of Ken Fielding's duties although he was still in the shadow of Fielding when it came to the final decision making. Ken's office was just next door to Lopez's and rest assured Ken's blessing was still required when it came to final approval of a franchise. Mike's family had emigrated from the Philippines, and he was very grateful to have risen through the ranks at ENO. He was a stocky bloke who resembled the character Oddjob, the antagonist's right hand man from the James Bond flick *Goldfinger*. He admired Fielding who was his mentor.

Lopez advised that Shayne would need to attend a multi-unit seminar at headquarters in Milford before they would approve a transfer. This was in spite of the fact that Subway HQ did not require this attendance until a third store was to be acquired. We marched on. On July 27, the rebel attended the multi-unit course, which, as it turned out, was of great value.

The January meeting to protest Suzanne Greene's mystery approval of her new store did result in some changes. Shane Menard replaced Steve Green as our field consultant in Bridgenorth. Menard arrived with a reputation for flirting and making passes at female employees. It had been reported and subsequently confirmed that he had made unwarranted advances toward Flo Card some years before.

Our sales, customer counts, and profitability were soaring. Nevertheless, his compliance reports conveyed an entirely different perception. It seemed like he had been instructed to come down hard on us based on the large discrepancy between his and Green's evaluations.

In the meantime, Lopez delayed our purchase application, citing mix-ups in paperwork and various other menial details, even though Shayne had attended the multi-unit course in July as directed. Lopez was successful in pushing the transfer to the back burner. The Cooks decided to ask for an increase in price from $175,000 to $192,500. We couldn't blame them for upping the ante as their sales were rising and seven months had passed since the offer in February. Shayne agreed to the increased price, and finally on February 25, 2004, nearly thirteen months after his original offer had been accepted, the store was transferred to us.

These are the projections and notes Shayne analyzed before presenting our offer to the Cooks:

	Cook Actual (2003) 2003		Randall Projected (2004)	
Sales	410,000		450,000	+8%
Cost	(169,000)	41%	(144,000)	32%
Gross	241,000	58%	306,000	
Expenses				
Accounting/Legal	2991		1,800	
Advertising/Promotion	23,493		21,000	
Automobile	2453		2,000	
Bank Charges	676		800	
Insurance	96		875	
Office/Postage	8,328		1,500	
Rent/Cam.	20,56		20,561	
Repairs/Maintenance	4,057		4,800	
Subway 8% Royalties	32,800		36,000	
Telephone/Internet	766		1,000	
Utilities	7,366		7,735	
Wages/Benefits	103,176	(25.1%)	76,500	(17%)
	(207,628)		(178,205)	
Net	**33,372**		**127,795**	

Shayne's projection of a 10% decrease in food costs coupled with an 8% increase in sales would prove to be an accurate estimate. Add to that a reduction in wage expenses of 8%, and this store was astoundingly more profitable than before we arrived.

Without exception, when we took over a new store, food costs would immediately decrease because our family was watching. It's difficult to steal food when a family member is always looking over your shoulder. Labour costs also decreased as we became more productive with employee effectiveness.

LANDLORDS AND LEASES

Our landlord in Bridgenorth was a grizzled Italian contractor in his 70s named Bruno DeMarchi. Tough yet fair, he was aware of all the problems that would arise at our building on an ongoing basis and was quick to solve them. Our relationship was terrific. Subway HQ is the lessee on all rental agreements. In our case, Ken Fielding Enterprises interfaces with the local landlords, negotiates terms and conditions, and seeks the approval from the franchisee. Once the landlord, ENO, and the franchisee are on the same page, Subway HQ executes the lease. Most leases are for five years, with two subsequent five-year options. Once they negotiate terms and conditions with landlords, Subway sublets the premises to the franchisee. This method insures that Subway always controls the location of their franchises, and this is a common occurrence in the fast food industry. Over ten years, we listened to over one hundred inquiries concerning a franchise transfer of one of our three stores. Subway is expert in lease negotiations yet, in spite of this, whenever we entertained inquiries from prospective buyers over the years, the first question asked was always, "How much is the rent?" The question that should have been asked was, "How profitable is your store?"

Changing pace from the kindly landlord we had in Bridgenorth, our new location on Chemong Road was owned by one of the largest commercial realtors in Canada. The difference was night and day. While Bruno would respond to a phone call immediately, Capital Property Management, the new landlord, took weeks or even months to respond. Two years after we sold the Chemong Road location, Capital Property Management was still mailing us a stream of useless information. Theirs was more of a bureaucracy than a business.

There are some obvious advantages to having two locations. Sharing staff, product, and management created profitable synergies, but two stores meant twice as many headaches. By the spring of 2004, we had a decent store manager in Bridgenorth, which only offset the loss of my brother Kent who was attending the University of Waterloo and living in Kitchener. The new store had a fully trained staff, and as was always the case in these changeovers, they would all be gone after the first ninety days. We were more prepared for this transition than we were with our first store. With almost four years experience and five family members involved, we were ready to enjoy the increased sales and profits that these two locations would offer. One advantage was the ability to stage and deliver our school orders from the Chemong location, which was more centrally located to the school customers.

With the purchase of the Chemong Road store came an obligation to renovate to the upgraded "Tuscany" décor. We were located in a small strip plaza on a busy arterial road at a key intersection. A new Canadian Tire had been built across the street and a Wal-Mart Superstore was to be relocated and upgraded to sit adjacent to it.

We were next door to a Tim Horton's, which was to be relocated one mile south. Upon learning of this, Shayne contacted the landlord inquiring if he could move his store into the space the coffee shop had vacated. It provided more square footage and was situated in a more favourable location at the end of the strip mall, facing the east and north. As was always the case when dealing with Capital Property Management, months passed before there was any meaningful dialogue. Our refurbishing date had long passed, and Subway was pushing for the Tuscany décor upgrade.

However, they understood that relocation and décor upgrade should be simultaneous. During this process, Steve Green and Shane Menard had come and gone, supplanted by a third FC named Barb Pineau who for some reason was headquartered in Sudbury, Ontario, 200 miles north of Peterborough.

Pineau's evaluations did account for the age of the Chemong Road store and the fact that renovations were forthcoming. That lenient stance changed over time to a no tolerance directive from ENO.

Although fluent in both French and English, the writing in her evaluation reports left our staff perplexed, as it was very confusing. She fit the pattern of ENO's other field consultants who were limited in interpersonal and communication skills.

When Shayne finally met with Capital Property, he was advised that our strip plaza (containing six stores) was to be demolished and replaced by a revamped adjacent building. To our delight, Subway was able to negotiate an excellent lease, increase our square footage, and secure the corner location we desired, which offered a full view of traffic from both sides. This relocation of course would exceed the proposed cost and completion date but was great news for the future success of this Subway location. It would turn out to be the most attractive Subway location in the region, and sales increased 25% the day it opened.

EMPLOYEE EXPECTATION

The employees we inherited at our second location would, of course, not remain with us very long. You can always count on a worker's revolt when new owners arrive. The employees will always perceive new ideas as inferior and can become quite enraged when change is employed. It angers them. They are comfortable and think they are pretty good at what they do. The credentials you bring mean nothing to staff that are not at ease with any changes, even small ones.

Two weeks after acquiring the Chemong Road store, Shayne arrived at 9:00 a.m. one day to find three employees having a smoke break at the back door. They had timed in at 8:45 a.m. and immediately took a break. Our custom was that management paid for breaks, and it wasn't necessary to time in and out. It was acknowledged that they would be taken when the flow of customers allowed. When Shayne reminded these three that he was paying them to have a break before they had performed a minute of work, they became quite annoyed and accused him of spying on them as he had arrived unannounced. Little wonder that a 100% turnover in staff occurs within ninety days of new management at Subway. Although the Ontario labour law requires two weeks' notice of employment termination, the same is not required of employees if they choose to quit. Another employee did not show up for work and had his roommate call in the next day to inform that he was quitting. Cultivating a good staff relationship is important, but remember, staff have no obligation to ownership. It is important to remember that when you terminate employees you need to be mindful of the rules but end the relationship on your terms, not the employee's.

"Years ago, I learned not to be totally dependant on my staff." My dad explains. "The reality is that as a franchisee you often have to account personally for your staff's shortcomings, short tempers, and in particular their absences. There is no one waiting in the wings to help in an emergency, no 'call a sandwich artist' temp service."

In July of 2004, Peterborough had its second hundred-year storm in five years. I guess Al Gore was right about the unpredictability of climate change. This was worse than the previous storm and created havoc throughout the community. The main street, George, became a river with jet-skis racing down its length. We kept both stores open through this event, short-staffed and overworked because we were two of very few restaurants operating during the flood. Late in the day, one of our female employees at the Chemong Road location, at the end of her patience, threw a punch in my old man's direction, after he made what he thought was a simple request. He ducked in time realizing that there is only so much an employee can tolerate. She had been pushed too hard. Shayne drove her home, happy that she didn't have a bread knife in her hand when she decided to throw that haymaker. Fast food customer service is a difficult, multitask occupation. Many people are incapable of adjusting to its constant demands. Even the best of workers has a breaking point.

FRANCHISE TERMINATION

In the summer of 2004, as we transitioned to a two-store enterprise, sales in our original Bridgenorth location continued to flourish thanks to family and a hard-working conscientious staff. We were achieving consistent weekly year-to-year gains of 15-20%, compared to the ENO average of 3.5%. Our school lunch program was a success. But most importantly, we had recovered our original purchase investment in thirty months. In spite of this, Shane Menard's inspections reflected a different story.

Fast-food store inspections are not unlike judging in figure skating or Olympic diving. They are susceptible to subjective interpretation and tampering. The difference is that in those sports, there are six to eight judges. We in the Subway sandwich business let our fate dangle on the judgment of one. This sole individual can spell the difference between success and failure for a franchisee. If Menard decided, for whatever reason, the baked bread was not to his standard, even if the people working did not understand why the bread was characterized as less than stellar, he could mark us out of compliance. And if you disagreed, rest assured the next visit he would mark us out again for our bread baking or whatever compliance indiscretion he could extrapolate from his bag of tricks. If he marked us out three months in a row, a crisp letter of termination would arrive at our door. In hindsight, had we cultivated a fawning relationship with Menard, maybe we could have avoided such strict evaluations.

On July 12, 2004, he marked us out of compliance in Bridgenorth for a third month in a row, even though he had only been our field consultant for five months and our sales were growing. He couldn't find much good to say about our operation, and we had nothing positive to report on him either. This was in stark contrast to Steve Green who had progressively marked us as an improving store and seldom out of compliance. It had become apparent to us that each ENO field consultant did not mark stores consistently.

We promptly received a letter of termination. This was followed by a probation agreement that would in effect allow us to redeem ourselves, and if successful be re-instated as franchisees. The agreement specified that if we maintained a "non-compliance free" store for 3 months, all sins would be forgiven, and we would be released from the penalty box and reinstated as a franchisee. We had no choice but to pay some legal fees ($850), sign the agreement, and embrace Menard for three months.

The consequences of franchise termination were never explained in layman's terms to Shayne or me until years later. In hindsight, we should have been more inquisitive before signing the arbitration agreement on August 19, 2004. It is a draconian intimidation tactic that is dishonourable and arguably dishonest. However, only a fool would try to argue against this action in court, not against Subway's deep pockets. The mountain of paperwork you sign when becoming a franchisee leaves an owner without much recourse. The adversarial rapport between Shayne and Menard was a seemingly inevitable dynamic, but in retrospect, had Shayne toned down his "in your face" questioning of Menard's grading of our store, he may have avoided them using this tactic or maybe not.

DOUBLE TROUBLE

In 2004, two stores afforded advantages and disadvantages. Our staff at Bridgenorth was efficient and hard-working, which resulted in higher traffic and startling increases. Menard's monthly inspections indicated an obvious deviation from reality. His evaluations concluded that we were doing more things wrong than right. Real-life indicators told the actual story.

Friendly staff, satisfied customers, increased profits, and a booming school-lunch program provided us our own realistic evaluation. Shayne had experienced an increasing number of inquiries from different parties expressing interest in purchasing the Bridgenorth store. Of these parties, most had visited many other locations and concluded that we were one of the top stores in the area. The Poobah and his band could not refute the reality that their flawed inspection reports belied.

ENO would voicemail a report each Friday called a download report. It profiled the previous week's sales totals for the four separate territories in the ENO umbrella. The Peterborough district is comprised of thirty stores and each week the voicemail download report would herald the top three stores by sales volume. Usually the big population area stores led the way. In 2004, ENO changed the reporting method to fall in line with Subway's WISR, which emphasized sales increases, year to year. With these new parameters, our stores would now have their percentage increases reported. For the next few years, Bridgenorth and Chemong were almost exclusively in the top three.

Our staff in Bridgenorth included two sisters who would later purchase one of our locations. In his reports, Menard had intimated that we were poor trainers, but once again, history would prove him wrong as these ladies would eventually become model franchisees in the eyes of ENO. It helped that they were young, unassuming, and, along with their parents, projected a benign attitude towards their new partnership. They heeded Shayne's "Don't get in ENO's face" advice, and their subsequent inspections were always positive. They immediately became favourites of ENO despite our purported poor training.

We owned these two locations simultaneously for only fifteen months but learned conclusively that two stores was the worst scenario. We were too small for a second tier of management but too stretched for our single tier to perform fluidly. Thanks to Jared Fogel, Subway's brand awareness boomed, profits rose, and those gains eased the stress. Add to that the impending relocation and building of a new store. As more suitors for the Bridgenorth store approached Shayne, Menard actually marked us in compliance three months in a row, sufficient to release us from our franchise limbo.

Early in 2005, we faced a crossroads as we entertained unsolicited offers for the Bridgenorth store. Our location on Chemong Road offered a big upside in sales and needed relocation and refurbishing. The family workforce was diminishing as Kent was attending university in Waterloo. Proving how valuable experienced Subway sandwich artists are, he was hired on the spot by a franchisee three blocks from his residence. Back in Peterborough, we were five years into our odyssey. The two stores were experiencing sales increases of 20% each. However, it was more like owning two and a half stores. We had collectively agreed that in our Subway careers we were closer to the end than the beginning. The bloom had left the rose, and a sale of the Bridgenorth operation seemed logical and timely.

THE SALE TO WICKS

Along came Chris Wicks, a jovial and thoughtful individual who was keen to acquire the Bridgenorth location. He made a generous offer, performed his due diligence with great vigour, and after he and his wife completed a successful outing at Subway University, they took over operations on June 1, 2005. He took only ten weeks to complete the transfer, which is extremely fast.

Once the changeover occurred, Wicks confided to Shayne that ENO brass had told him not to take any advice from Shayne because he had a reputation as a rebel and a loose cannon. Shayne took back a mortgage that Wicks paid promptly every month until he suddenly sold the location fourteen months later. He had become a shadow of his former eager and ebullient self. He wasn't the same man who had just recently signed on for what he thought would be a long and exciting endeavour. Unable to tolerate the demands of Menard and the rest of the ENO's staff, he wanted out at all costs, to "get his life back" he said. His timing was perfect as he sold his store for $340,000 ($80,000 more than he had paid us just over a year prior). He sold to Raj Ballah, who was acquiring his second store and was becoming a favourite franchisee of Fielding and his staff. Ballah fit the Fielding's qualifications to a tee, and as we were finding out, Subway HQ's as well.

Our agenda was easier now, as we could concentrate on the relocation and the refurbishing assignment at Chemong and work on increasing sales. Somewhere near the end of 2005, we decided that we would embark on a new direction. We were tiring of the

Subway life, had achieved our goals, and were now looking forward to completing the renovations and showcasing the store to possible buyers. While it still had an upside, the family's energy for Subway was depleting. My brother Nolan would be off to college soon, Kent was pursuing a career in Urban Planning, and I had just graduated from Trent and was searching for other opportunities.

BIG BOSS MAN

From the beginning of our association with Subway, Shayne was impressed with its system of recording and monitoring its franchisees. Every week, we were emailed a WISR (Weekly Inventory and Sales Report), which tracks every franchisee's sales and displays weekly, monthly, and yearly statistics. It compares results among all stores within the ENO jurisdiction (230 locations as of September 2009) and is an excellent barometer of where your store is ranked. This recording and reporting system was the constant that Shayne and I used to measure success or failure over the years. Not surprisingly, it was used as a barometer when prospective buyers assessed one of our stores. It is a Subway HQ report that is like a rudder that steers your franchise. We loved the information it provided.

ENO holds operations meetings every six months, usually in the centrally located town of Huntsville, Ontario. This is a chance to bring franchisees up to speed on past, present, and future Subway happenings. The meeting usually commences with a state of the union address from Fielding. These meetings were draining in that they didn't seem to provide very much new information or ideas that we could take back to Peterborough. Some parts were useful, but the meetings could have been condensed to one day. On a few occasions, trade shows were provided, which gave suppliers a chance to showcase their latest products and franchisees an opportunity to decide what products they wanted to sell at their respective stores. These portions of the meetings were constructive and made the franchisee feel like they had some autonomy, or at least a hand, in the decision-making process. The drive to Huntsville, through beautiful Northern Ontario land-scapes, was the biggest highlight of these trips.

When awards for achievement were presented, they were given to Fielding's favourites rather than the ones who deserved them. In 2005, when our school lunch program had grown to serve fourteen schools, he presented the school lunch program award. It was given to an area franchisee that supplied two school lunches each month. When Shayne inquired, Menard said that our record of fourteen school lunches was not considered because we did not report these lunches properly. We had reported them exactly as instructed, and they were confirmed by our head office co-coordinator, Barb McMellon.

Fielding's outlook trickled all the way down to his field consult-ants. They became obstructers rather than mentors, destroyers of morale as opposed to confidence builders. Their attitude was to catch and scold when it should have been to suggest and improve. It would take a minimum of two days after an Evaluation and Compliance Review to repair staff morale. It is hard to fathom that other DAs within the Subway system operated in the same fashion as Fielding.

THE EVALUATION PROCESS

A typical monthly Evaluation and Compliance Review would take a field consultant two hours to perform. The FC would come in unannounced and inspect and rate the restaurant on a multitude of categories including:

- Customer Service
- Product Quality and Food Safety
- Record Keeping and Profitability
- Baking Procedures
- Cleanliness
- Equipment and Storage

Within these categories were countless items that were inspected and rated. Various points were assigned to arrive at a percentage total. It is a tedious and complicated assessment of each restaurant's practices. Over our decade, it was always a moving target that vaguely used the Subway Operations Manual as a guideline and was always subject to a single person's analysis. If you were marked non-compliant by that solitary judge, there was no recourse, no second observation from another FC, no second opinion so to speak. This was the only flaw in an otherwise impressive Subway methodology. Other Quick Serve Restaurants (QSR) franchisors such as A&W, McDonald's, and Tim Hortons, do not monitor their franchisees as intensely or as frequently.

Every franchisor has an internal evaluation system in place to protect their brand name. Subway sends field consultants into stores every month to inspect the store and evaluate performance. They are supposed to analyze all facets of the business such as health code regulations, cleanliness, customer service, food quality preparation, uniform policy, and general Subway regulations.

We have discovered over the years that our relationship with various FCs have affected our standing in the evaluation process and possibly created a bias against us that would make it increasingly difficult to effectively run our stores without the fear of having them taken away. In many instances, their judgment affected our ability to run our stores with continued efficiency. When I became an owner, I knew this was going on so I made efforts to impress Barb Pineau. It seemed to work. She appeared to like me and marked our store fairly for the first year or so. It wasn't until a certain incident involving a mousetrap that she began to change her tune and began to remember that, even as nice and accommodating as I may have appeared to be, I would never be able to escape the stigma of the Randall name.

If an FC marks your store out of compliance in any of these categories for three consecutive months you receive a termination letter. In almost four years of Green's tenure, we were seldom marked out of compliance. As I have mentioned earlier, when Menard arrived in April of 2004, he rarely marked us in compliance. We thought we had improved immensely since our start, as sales seemed to verify. We received a termination of franchise letter in August of 2004 and asked to sign an arbitration agreement.

The second and final time this occurred was in 2009. We had been marked out of compliance many times over the previous year, but suddenly we were told we violated our probation and would have to go to arbitration. The terms of compliance were so ambiguous, we did not really understand why all of the sudden we were being taken into probation considering we had had rougher patches over the years. The terms and conditions of an arbitration agreement are best explained by a lawyer. But Shayne signed the agreement, confident we could placate Menard and get a clean bill of health. We eventually became compliant, paid some legal fees as a penalty, and looked on the incident as part of the Subway experience. It wasn't important to us as sales were growing, which seemed to contradict the investigation and the whole arbitration process. Unsolicited prospective buyers were lining up and when Menard heard that we were considering a sale of the franchise, his evaluations suddenly became much more flattering. The Chemong store was in compliance during this arbitration process, but, in our opinion, did not perform as well as Bridgenorth. The lesson learned is that whether or not these rules are fully enforced depends on your personal standing with your field consultants and their superiors. Once the process gets to arbitration, you are all but dead. You enter a kangaroo court situation where you state your case and the Subway legal department states theirs. Guess who wins that debate? Subway is covered by all the paperwork signed upon closing the deal to buy the store. Pages upon pages of contracts that allow them to operate in such fashion where they are able to force an owner to forfeit his or her store at any given time based on the judgment of a solitary field consultant or the orders of his or her superiors. The relationship between the franchisee and the DA's organization must be given close attention.

A few years into owning his first store, Shayne hired Sara and Caryn Blake, who ended up being two of the best employees we ever had. They were loyal, trustworthy, reliable, and productive. The relationship was so good that we ended up selling our second store to their family and the two sisters became franchisees. The transaction was probably the most satisfying of any we had because of whom he sold it to and the affect it would have on their family. We trained these girls; they parlayed those skills into becoming excellent franchisees. There was an ENO meeting shortly after the sale where we sat at the same table as these young women and watched them accept an award for the amount of Subway University courses completed by their employees. Subway University is an online program offering information and examination sessions that are worthwhile training aids. They include over 200 categories and are a good tool towards success-fully running a Subway franchise. The bulk of those courses were completed while Shayne was the owner, in large part due to an incentive program he created that actually paid employees to complete the courses. ENO gave the Blakes an award for the number of Subway University courses completed. We didn't receive an award.

Fast forward to 2007. When Shayne sold to the Blake sisters, they were getting the most promising store in the area with the most potential. He had just completed renovations that greatly enhanced the store's potential with a new location and overall appearance. It was now on the corner of a newly constructed building with excellent sight lines for drivers arriving from all directions near the busy intersection. The road to the east was second busiest traffic artery in Peterborough.

Upon the transfer of any store, the field consultant must ascertain what the seller needs to replace or repair so that the store is in good standing for the takeover. The renovations were completed in July of 2007, and the store was sold eleven months later. During that time, the store was in compliance and had relatively no issues. Two weeks before the sale, the FC decided we needed a new Point of Sale system, two new microwaves, and an overhaul of the freezer. The total cost was $7,000. This was a brand new restaurant. Incidentally, after purchasing the new microwaves and having no use for the old ones, Shayne lent them to a nearby Subway whose own microwaves had broken down. The same FC inspected that store while our old microwaves, that weren't fit to use while in our store, were being used.

Conversely, when we were buying a store, the state of the store we were taking over didn't seem to require such improvements. We bought our third store, which at the time was fourteen years old and had never been renovated. We ended up spending a substantial sum in renovations, which should have been the obligation of the seller. Within the first year of purchasing the Parkhill store, we spent $35,000 in improvements that by ENO's standards should have been the responsibility of the previous owners.

Ideally, one would like to assume that each field consultant marks his or her stores in the same fashion, with the same criteria as every other FC. After all, Subway is a company that wants to protect its brand name with consistent, thorough monitoring of the execution of their business model. During our tenure, we had three different field consultants with three different perspectives on marking a store. Each one had certain focuses that appeared important to them while other areas were not scrutinized as much.

CROSSROADS

In October 2005, I drove my dad to Buffalo to catch a plane due south for Tampa Bay. He was visiting my older brother Kyle. On the way down and on the subsequent drive back we talked about our future with Subway. It was becoming harder to stay in compliance. The pressure was wearing us thin. We discussed our exit strategy from Subway and possible future ventures. On the return home, we stopped in Toronto, visiting a bustling restaurant that the owner was considering franchising. Later that fall, we investigated a golf merchandising operation. We resolved that we would be vigilant in watching for new opportunities.

Barb Pineau, a field consultant from the Sudbury area, had replaced Menard. We passed her inspections that summer and fall, and during that winter our new premises, a renovated location that we would move into soon, was being constructed. Shayne accumulated a war chest to provide our portion of the $125,000 relocation. The vision was to spare no expense in making the finished product the best Subway anywhere.

Shayne and I continued to explore new business opportunities that summer as sales and profitability continued upward. We were fortunate that we had never experienced a downturn in profit. During our worst stretch, the lowest sales increase we had was 4% during the renovations at Chemong. We would like to say it was solely a product of our superior technique but much was a result of luck and timing. While sales continued to show increases over the previous year, our Evaluation and Compliance Reviews were not as encouraging. We were marked more severely than ever despite our experience in the business.

At this point, to protect ourselves, we made a concerted effort to try to stay in compliance. Every request made by our FC was dispatched promptly with regard to improvement to our store. Hopefully this would bring us into a better standing.

When we visited other Subway franchises, we usually confirmed that our store was operating proficiently by comparison, though our field consultants' reviews suggested otherwise.

Many of our employees over the years had experience working at other Subway stores throughout the ENO territory. During our ten years, these employees would frequently comment on how they believed we ran efficient stores that were at least equal or more efficient than the other stores they had worked at. People like Eric Ingram, Michelle Scott, Sara Blake, Angie Verheem, Michael Hay, and Shannon Coccozolli, just to name a few, would commonly remark on how our FC inspections were noticeably stricter than what they had experienced at different stores.

FAMILIES FROM AFAR

The Indian influx was now in full bloom and with Subway adding fewer new locations, resale prices were accelerating. What used to be a selling price of 45% of annual gross sales had risen to around 85%, with bidding among suitors becoming commonplace.

One of the challenges facing a prospective Subway buyer is that if they are Canadian or American they have to compete with stores run by Indian immigrants who are able to fill them with family members, whose wages might be lower than average, which in turn greatly skews the productivity figures. They have the advantage of paying their family members lower wages and overstaffing without worrying about high labour expenses. Outside of food costs, labour costs are a store's biggest expense and can greatly affect profitability.

The Indian presence in the Subway franchisee community has greatly affected the process of prospective buyers. When Shayne started in 2000, there were few Indian franchisees. Back in early 2007 when I went to the two-week Subway training course in Milford, Connecticut, during a break period I looked at the names on the attendance sheet and deduced that 80% of my fellow students were from India. Many Indian franchisees who own multiple stores and have large families back home, will buy stores knowing they can fully staff them with family members who are chomping at the bit to move to North America and start a new life. They typically do not have as many problems with staffing in regards to high labour costs, training costs, or employee unrest, which make their stores more profitable, and thusly they are able to acquire multiple stores faster. Because they are willing to pay more, the purchase prices have risen accordingly, leaving fewer domestic buyers with the wherewithal to enter the Subway industry.

Subway's brand name has become bigger and stronger over the last decade, the combination of its great reputation and the flood of immigrant owners who have driven the value of stores up dramatically. Shayne bought his first store in 2000 for 40% of the store's gross sales. Before we sold our final store, we had an offer for 92% of the gross sales, which was a common selling percentage by then. The percentage had risen, and we were benefiting. We purchased our stores at reasonable prices and due to timing and circumstances were able to sell them at very high prices. To continue buying would have been difficult at these newly elevated prices. Without possessing a significantly large family workforce, we could not capitalize on the profit gained from the consequent low labour costs. We were also not interested in owning a store for an indefinite period, as one of our main criteria for buying such a business was its potentially short-term return on investment.

Another factor in this foreign buyer versus domestic buyer scenario is that Canadians do not value work as much as in my grandfather's time and family businesses started and staffed by Canadians have become a distant memory. Ours was technically a family business but unlike most Indian franchisees, we had an end game. My brothers and I never had any intention of sticking with Subway forever and neither did our old man for that matter.

PART III

AN OFFER WE COULDN'T REFUSE

By the fall of 2006, Shayne and I were pondering our next move, whether it was to sell Chemong and get out of the business completely or build a new store. After proposing a few ideas for start-up projects in new locations, Mike Lopez (now Vice President of Operations) declined every one of them down saying that, in each instance, the traffic flow wasn't sufficient enough to support a new store. We believed him. Opportunities for acquiring another existing store were scarce as none were up for sale.

At this point, I was managing Chemong while Shayne and Beverly were emergency staff and didn't work regular shifts. They took responsibility for the making and delivery of the school lunches, the platter catering, and the deliveries. We didn't offer a delivery service but, on occasion, would make an exception. Shayne was also on call when we ran out of product between our twice-weekly food deliveries from our supplier Sysco Foods. He would borrow from nearby Subways, a common occurrence when we experienced sales increases.

On one sparkling autumn morning, Shayne visited the Subway on Parkhill Road to return borrowed product. Shawna Cleary, who along with her sister Deanna was the store's franchisee, mentioned to Shayne that they were selling the store and were meeting a prospective buyer that very afternoon. Shayne suggested that he and I might be interested in purchasing their store. Her location was open twenty-four-hours, 364 days out of the year and was located at a busy intersection. It catered to Trent University students who inhabited much of the surrounding neighbourhood. It was a rough area that sported drug dealers and a known crack house a few doors down. Nonetheless, it did volume close to $950,000 annually.

My dad called me up that day and pitched the idea of us buying the Cleary store. We agreed that we were in a much different mode than we were six years before, and our allegiance to Subway was wearing thin. I was more interested in leaving Subway, specifically ENO, and was motivated to start a fresh new venture. The only thing keeping me from leaving was the appeal of this new store and the financial opportunity it offered. Finding someone to loan me the money to become a partner at this new store meant, as a twenty-five-year old fresh out of university, I could make a good deal of money in a short period of time.

Shayne and I met with Shawna and her father Peter Cleary the next day to discuss the possibility of a transfer. Shayne describes it as, "the most pleasant occurrence of his entire Subway experience." The price offered was $500,000, and they would agree to take back a mortgage of $150,000 at 7% amortized over sixty months. They provided us with WISRs and financial statements, and we agreed to meet again within twenty-four hours. The meeting only took thirty minutes, surprising considering we were discussing a fairly sizable purchase.

The subsequent examination of the financial statements justified the proposed selling price. It calculated at 54% of sales, a huge bargain in the current market.

The big question was how could we supply the effort to man and operate a twenty-four-hour operation when our zest was waning and ENO's pressure on us intensifying? Our logic was if we could operate this store for a minimum of two years, we could resell at that juncture and take advantage of Canadian tax laws. We also anticipated that we could increase sales and get a resale price of at least 75% of sales. In addition, we would repay much of the $500,000 purchase price by our resale date target. The downside was that operating an around-the-clock store required a special effort, but we would face the challenge. We would be operating two stores once again.

DUSK TIL DAWN

By October 2006, we were in solid shape financially. When we sold the Bridgenorth store to Chris Wicks, we retired the outstanding purchase debt on the Chemong store, paying off the Cook mortgage and a small loan we had with the bank. Shayne and I decided we would attempt to finance the Parkhill purchase in full without using any of our own capital. We had been using a bank in a minor way over the years and had an agreement in place to finance the Chemong Road relocation that was coming soon. Scotiabank had agreed to provide funding for $100,000 toward the refurbishment. We approached them to participate in our purchase of the Parkhill Road franchise. They agreed to fund $175,000 of the purchase price with Cleary willing to take on $150,000. We required another $175,000 to complete the transaction. God bless the credit card companies.

We would never recommend a purchase of a franchise with 100% credit leverage. This was a unique situation, and the stars were aligned for the "lucky bastard" once again.

We financed the balance with various credit card interest rates from 1.9%-12%. These did not have any special requirements and no guarantees other than keeping the balances current and paying the interest due. In the final analysis, we were able to execute the purchase of the Parkhill Subway without expending a dime of Randall capital.

After analyzing Parkhill's financial statements, we created the following income statement:

PROJECTION —PARKHILL SUBWAY

Sales	952,350	(5% INCREASE)
Food Costs	(276,080)	(29% OF SALES)
Net	676,270	

Expenses

Advertising/Promotion (5%)	6,000
Bank Charges	47,600
Insurance	4,000
Legal/Accounting	1,000
Office Postage	2,500
Rent	500
Repairs/Maintenance	32,000
Subway 8% Royalties	7,500
Telephone/Internet	76,188
Utilities Vehicle/Travel	3,500
Wages	140,000
	<337,788>
Net	**338,482**

MY TREK TO MILFORD

Once we made a firm offer to the Cleary family, the transaction had one stumbling block. When meeting with ENO on December 5, 2006, Mike Lopez insisted that I be a co-franchisee and therefore would have to make the drive to Milford and take the two-week training course, despite my seven years experience at Subway. This was not an unreasonable request, considering Shayne was now sixty-four.

So, in February of 2007, I set off for Milford. It was a ten-hour odyssey that saw me fear for my life as my feathery Hyundai Accent, devoid of snow tires, hovered over the interstate during a two-hour blizzard. I arrived at my hotel shaking like a recovering alcoholic experiencing cold sweats. Withstanding the storm served as a precursor to the tempest of obstacles that would rain down on us as we embarked on our third and final store. It was the first Sunday in February and for the first time since I could remember I missed the bulk of the Super Bowl. I made it for the fourth quarter, but by then, the Colts had it locked up. Not an auspicious beginning to what would surely be a grinding two weeks. Subway University's role was to see how much knowledge it could provide to me after seven years of operating two different Subway franchises. Although redundant in many areas, the experience was very interesting and imparted insight and knowledge that I did not have when I arrived. It had also confirmed that the Indian infusion was worldwide as over 80% of my class of around one hundred trainees was of that origin. In this sense, ENO's franchisees were reflective of Subway franchisees across the world.

There was a sharp contrast between the teaching methods of Subway Headquarters and ENO. The difference was their professionalism, knowledge, communication skills, and most importantly, the respect they gave us. They were there to train us, and it actually resembled a university setting with classes, workshops, tests, and at the end, a written exam. Whereas HQ was engaged in trying to make us better franchisees by facilitating a more positive learning environment, ENO tended to be aloof and domineering. At that stage, with my experience, I knew more than most did in the class but still gained knowledge that I would take back with me to Ontario. Even though I knew our DA did not operate at the same level as the instructors in Milford, I still hoped, for the sake of my classmates who would be operating in different regions around the world that their future DAs operated at a similarly high level.

There were people from all over the world being trained, mostly couples. There was one from Greece, another from Sweden, and two young blokes from Belfast, who were the only two in the class younger than I was. I quickly befriended the Irishmen. The hardest working students in the class were the remaining 80%, who were from India.

The method of conduct Fielding has developed over the years is predicated on the need—as it should be for any DA in the world—to keep his franchisees doing things the right way. His theory is that the best way to ensure store owners are following the rules is to scare them in the same way a high school football coach tries to motivate his players. The only problem is that it has a different affect on adults than it does on teenagers. Nonetheless, it seems to work for Fielding who has been heralded by Subway as one of its finest development agents.

At one of ENO's semi-annual meetings, an entire hour was

spent where Ken Fielding sat on a stage and took part in a "this is your life" presentation performed by his staff, who have great respect for their boss. The presentation expanded on how he got into the business, his successes, and the courtship of his wife, while the crowd of franchisees watched. There were a few yawns.

This was by far the happiest I ever saw Ken Fielding. He was as comfortable as Kim Jong-il having his golf scorecard marked by a member of his staff. If you haven't heard, the diminutive North Korean leader shot a world record 38 under-par with five holes-in-one in his first round ever played. This comparison in no way insinuates that Fielding's finger was or is dangling over the nuclear bomb button; he's not that nefarious.

The ENO meetings would commonly take place over two days, but easily could have been condensed into one had the content been stripped to just essential information. The "this is your life" episode is only one example of something that could have been omitted. Another meeting had a police officer explain for two hours how to protect against fraud on your Interac machine (A machine that accepts direct payments from a bank account or credit payments from a customer through the use of a plastic swipe card). After the first twenty minutes, the remaining one hundred were superfluous.

On one occasion, the drive home was a little sweeter, as for just one transient moment at least, our luck with ENO had changed. There was a draw prize at the end of one of the meetings as people were standing, talking, all about to vacate the building. Amidst the commotion, Mike Lopez reached into a box and pulled out a piece of paper with a name on it. Before reading the name aloud he instinctively reacted, "Oh noooo . . . Shayne Randall . . . Shayne Randall isn't here, is he?...Has he left?...OK, I'll draw another name . . . no, he IS here? Jeez." Shayne walked up to accept the prize, a 40" flat screen TV, and Lopez completely ignored him.

THE STORE THAT NEVER SLEEPS

On February 21, 2007, we were the new owners of the Parkhill restaurant, embarking on our final chapter as Subway franchisees. We were surprised that the deal went through so expediently. The fact that the Cleary's were favourites of Fielding helped them when they wanted to sell. We had now owned each of the three franchises David Kjaer had pioneered and, as it would turn out, were the greatest benefactors of his efforts, at least financially.

It wasn't long before we realized why the Cleary's had seemingly given us such a generous deal. We were ready for the staff rebellion, the long hours, and the constant obstacles that ENO had in store for us, but we had no idea how much difference there would be in operating a store for 168 hours a week compared to the 103 we were used to. Until we sold the franchise in September of 2009, Shayne and I slept with one eye open, his blood pressure surged, and we both dreamed of the end. He would say, "The thirty-one months we owned this place felt like thirty-one years."

Back running two stores was nothing new, and we could enjoy the synergies once again. Looming though was the relocation of Chemong that was now only four months away. There wouldn't be much time to acquaint ourselves with our new digs, rehire and retrain staff, and acclimatize to a night and day operation. Although a good thing, our increased sales during this time required an efficient workforce, adding to the challenge. But as one employee said some seven years earlier, we would "get through it."

Eccentric characters never stopped walking through our doors. Being a twenty-four-hour store meant more of them at all times of the day. While there where many encounters that occurred during the night, two incidents that occurred during the day stick out in my mind.

One incident occurred when my mom was serving a sullen old lady who was in a wheelchair. The lady, a dead ringer for Madeline Albright, vociferously communicated exactly what was on her tired old mind. She was really upset that our sidewalk didn't have a ramp to help her wheelchair over the curb. My mother, intimidated, agreed that there should be a ramp and that she would inform the boss. Shayne happened to walk in while the lady was being served. The lady spotted Shayne and asked my mom if he was the owner to which she replied yes. Shayne noticed the lady's presence immediately upon entering the store, as most people would with such a character. The lady asked him, "Are you the boss?" Being a wise ass and wanting to avoid this woman, he replied, "No, she's the boss," and pointed at Beverly. The old lady's eyes lit up in a fury of anger. "You told me he was the boss! You are a piece of work. I'm never eating here again!"

For every anecdote about a customer encounter, there are another ten just as entertaining and another ten I've forgotten. At the very least, they keep you on your toes. The last one I'll tell you was not funny at all initially. It was disturbing and shook me up but as a few years have passed, I can laugh at it now. A man and his son, who was around five years old, came into the store during a quiet time just before dinner. I made them their subs, and cashed them in before they sat down and ate their subs in the restaurant. The man was playing with the son, and they seemed to be having a good time. However, the noise these two were making had escalated as the father was getting the son excited and wired. They sounded like a group of farm animals. I politely asked, "I'm sorry but would you guys mind keeping it down a little. Thanks."

There was no response. About five more minutes elapsed before they exited. I told them on their way out to, "Have a good night, guys." He put the kid in the car then furiously approached the door, opened it, and stuck his head in, "Shame on you, telling a laughing child to shut up, shame on you." His eyes were popping of his head like Malcolm McDowell's character in *A Clockwork Orange*. Then he gave me the finger and got into his car.

Fifteen minutes later, he re-entered the store. At this point, we were busy. He asked me for the manager, I said, "I'll do you one better, I'm the owner. What's the problem?" "There was no one here and you told us to shut up which meant we weren't offending anyone but YOU!" "Yes, you were bothering me. Do I not count?" "You told a five-year-old to shut up. The laughter of a child is sacred!" "I did not tell anyone to shut up. I don't have a problem with the child I have a problem with you. You're pretty worked up, and I'm sure you've got some other things going on, but this conversation is over. Please leave." "I only get to see him once a month. Get a life, loser!" "Leave!" Everyone in line was holding back laughter. One girl said she would tell my boss what had happened and vouch for me.

THE CLEARY LEGACY

The ENO attitude through the initial stretch at Chemong was somewhat different from normal, almost subdued. Barb Pineau was approaching our relocation of Chemong with a positive demeanour, suggesting insightful improvements to the floor plan and décor. She inherited inspection duties for the Parkhill store from our old friend Steve Green, whom we had as our first field consultant at our first store. Her helpfulness at Chemong became a distant memory when she completed her first Evaluation and Compliance Review of the Parkhill store. In the following two years at Parkhill, she insisted on a myriad of changes, all of which should have been performed by the outgoing ownership.

When a franchise transfer is completed, the field consultant must make a note of deficiencies and they must be rectified before closing. Green must have been blindfolded when he performed his last inspection of Parkhill. He noted that there was a crack in the sneeze guard that required replacement, which subsequently the Cleary's completed. As mentioned earlier, in the inspections that were later performed on Pineau's watch, we:

- refurbished the freezer ($3,000),
- replaced the lighting grid ($2,000),
- replaced open sign ($1,000),
- added a front refrigerated cabinet ($1,500),
- replaced the sandwich unit ($15,000),
- replaced the POS unit ($4,500)

- replaced the baking oven that was only three years old ($6,500),
- enclosed the wiring panel ($1,500)

There were many other changes ordered by Pineau, all of which should have been completed by the former owners before the transfer occurred. When Pineau's requests were completed, they totaled in excess of $35,000.

During the summer, the stark reality of running a twenty-four-hour operation at the Parkhill location became evident. With a couple of exceptions, the employees had proven to be disgruntled underachievers. The location itself was situated in a tough section of the city. Customers were a cross section of all demographics. However, from September to April they were mainly Trent students.

Being open all night attracted cabbies, cops, night-shifters, and all creatures nocturnal. Many of our night denizens were inebriated or stoned. Staffing on this shift proved critical and challenging. It required someone that could handle all situations. It took two years to build the night business to the point where we required two employees on duty the entire eight-hour shift. We should have staffed two from the beginning but it was really difficult finding people that could handle the job. Having two people working would have added security and safety, cleaning duties would have been much easier, and sales would have increased because customers would notice the added efficiency.

Initially we had a constant turnover of night workers and other unsettling situations that probably would not have occurred with two people working. So until we permanently had two employees on staff in the spring of 2009, we soldiered on with just one employee from 3:00 a.m. to 7:00 a.m. The biggest downside was that Shayne (now sixty-seven) was the emergency employee when the clock went past midnight. He slept for two years with one eye open, ready to spring when his cell phone rang, anticipating any kind of ridiculous story. Although he loathed this part of the job, we were both convinced that being open twenty-four hours would prove to be worthwhile monetarily. In hindsight, we were correct.

Shayne would always have the best encounters with customers because he had the shortest fuse. The twenty-four-hour store produced the most entertaining escapades, especially when he was working late at night or early in the morning. One time at about 2:00 a.m., there were about five customers in the store. The first one in line appeared to have been recently smoking crack-cocaine. She paid for her sub and before leaving, grabbed about eight bags of chips and hightailed it to the exit, slamming into the dead-bolted door like Wiley Coyote. A large man in line decided to call the police on his cell phone while sitting on the woman as if she was a Barcalounger. Two weeks later she arrived with a cheque for $10, a figure awarded to us by the court for retribution. In our decade as franchisees, this was as close as we ever came to an actual robbery attempt.

On another occasion, Shayne's blood pressure was surely boiling as a group of drunken university kids had come in and were making a lot of noise. He finally exclaimed in his trademark projective pitch, "Alright guys, I've got a proposition for you." And at sixty-seven, his voice bellowed over the collective sound of the group. "I will give away a free cookie to whoever can scream the loudest. But you have to do it outside, and miss, (pointing to a young lady) you are the judge." He ushered them outside and to the side of the building near the home of an annoying neighbour we had. The neighbour had complained that our food delivery truck, which would arrive at 5:00 a.m. twice a week, was making too much noise. Shayne knew this would piss her off. The kids screamed their lungs out, and someone consumed a cookie free of charge. They came back inside to eat and didn't make another peep. Neither did the neighbour.

There was another heavy load to carry by the end of the summer of 2007. September had arrived, and the students were back. This would help fill the coffers at Parkhill. Over at Chemong, the fall signaled back to school for the high school and elementary school kids, which meant preparing numerous school lunch orders. Kent had been a pivotal worker, returning from April to September to assist at Chemong, but would depart for his final year at university, and Dad was now collecting the old age pension.

RAGS TO RICHES AGAIN

ENO had over two hundred stores during much of our tenure. Talented energetic entrepreneurs ran these franchises and risked their hard-earned savings to purchase and build these ventures. Although the road Shayne travelled before becoming a Subway operator was unusual, I am certain other franchisees could relate interesting backgrounds as well.

As Shayne tells it, "When I was eight years old I became a newspaper carrier. I started small, with twenty-five customers, an easy daily chore that was predictable. I netted a small salary each week. To earn more, I needed more customers. More customers meant more labour, delivering and collecting from readers. As the route grew in numbers, so did the risk. Soon, I had receivables, as some customers were tardy paying or skipped. I needed helpers to ease the stress of delivering a large number of papers before the supper hour. I learned that when you rise from twenty-five customers to three hundred, you increase your risk. In life, we all have risk. The greater the risk, the greater the reward and the more complicated your life becomes dealing with the rewards. Most lottery winners are small-risk takers. Most are not prepared to handle large rewards. Usually they fritter away their windfalls.

"The journey I took, that finished as a Subway franchisee in May of 2000, started in 1950 when I embarked on my first business as a Toronto Star paper carrier. A risk was taken at every milepost throughout that half century. Although I was labeled a gambler many times along the way, I never questioned the moniker. We're all gamblers. The difference in us lies in the amount and degree of risk we can tolerate.

"In 1988, after countless start-ups and subsequent sales of a cross section of businesses, my family's net worth had grown to an amount nearing $10 million. From leasing to recycling, sports franchises to art galleries, I had scrambled my way from purchasing a paper route in 1950 for $20 to considering with partners a purchase of a multi-national company. To now be treated by our new partner, Ken Fielding, without any respect was another lesson learned. You are only as good as your last success, and I had not had many since those halcyon times of the 1980s. In 1991, as Bob Rae's NDP government abused their mandate, resulting in heavy body blows to the entrepreneurial sector in Ontario, I was forced to take the biggest gamble of my business career. It didn't go my way.

"As asset and property values plummeted, my family's net worth did as well. Partnerships and alliances were fragile then, and on a grey October morning, my bankers called my loans. Although I had prepared a promising repayment proposal, they decided to take a $6 million loss rather than trust someone who had in 1984 paid $1.4 million in interest to financial institutions. They were perilous times and bigger men than me would also fall. From a bankruptcy position in 1992, our family struggled through a bleak seven-year period, riding buses, eating Kraft dinner, borrowing from friends and relatives, and taking on any job to feed, clothe, and house the family.

"Though times were grim, the glass was still half full. The family was intact, schools were being attended, and we couldn't accumulate any debt because no one would lend to us. No one went to jail. Not many opportunities for meaningful work surfaced as my resume intimidated would-be employers. After all, who would hire someone in a middle management position that once had six hundred employees? I applied for three hundred jobs over a five-year period, yielding only two interviews. Then, quite suddenly, a lawsuit that I had kept alive through legal aid, showed some promise. One of my partner's that had pulled the rug out from under us in 1991 had decided to settle. We agreed to an amount much less than we would have gotten had we pushed through to trial.

"I learned through these years that my success was my own making. So in 1999, we set out to find a business that had enough promise to return us to our long ago paths that led us to achieve our goals. Here I found myself.

"So, as I listened to the Fielding during one of the bi-annual ENO meetings, I would survey the room knowing that many of my fellow franchisees had travelled through similar ups and downs and were likewise squirming as he lectured on. They were the real risk takers, putting their fate in his hands. I travelled home that day wondering if I had made the right decision in purchasing a Subway franchise only a few months earlier."

Although Shayne's route to becoming a Subway franchisee was unique, so is the case for many of the men and women who become franchisees. It is an opportunity that is attractive to people of a variety of ages, past career paths, and prior business experience.

CHEMONG RELOCATION

The Chemong Road store was to be moved a mere forty feet south. First Capital's restructuring project would seem to take forever when in reality it would take only twenty-four months. We reached the only semi-stress free window with our DA's office during the early months of 2007. I assumed a management role at Parkhill, while Chemong had established an impressive staff, which contributed to high sales figures.

I made a concerted effort, in my new role as a franchisee, to try to avoid the pitfalls with ENO that Shayne had suffered. Mostly, I wanted to maintain a good standing with our field consultant Barb Pineau. I wanted to cultivate that relationship because if it ever became negative, I knew the consequences would be severe based on what I had seen in the past. During all of her visits, I was gregarious and positive in our interactions in an effort to show that we were trying our best to do everything correctly, exactly as ENO wanted the store conducted. At no point did I question anything, just smiled and tried to be humourous when it was appropriate. It seemed I was successful in the beginning, and we had a great rapport. She even sent me a birthday card in both 2008 and 2009.

Shayne was busy preparing for the move, ordering equipment, coordinating with our contractor and avoiding any confrontation with ENO. As the moving date of July 6 approached, we had set a goal to avoid any interruption in our restaurant service to our customers. Fortunately, we were able to continue in our location up until the day we would move. Our location displayed 95% brand new décor and equipment. Inventory was all that needed to be physically transferred.

On the evening of July 5, we closed as usual at 11:00 p.m. and opened 8:00 a.m. the next morning in our new location. We welcomed customers to what we thought was arguably the nicest looking Subway in Central Ontario. Customers echoed that sentiment as sales immediately grew by 25%. As usual, we failed to receive any congratulations from ENO.

This locale had tremendous potential. It was situated in the middle of the city's fastest growing shopping district. Two new housing projects were being built close by, providing accommodation for approximately three hundred families. Banks, beer and liquor stores, Wal-Mart, Canadian Tire, McDonald's, Wendy's, and Arby's were all close neighbours. Combine everything, the location, the upgrade, a competent staff, an 11:00 p.m. closing time, and we were feeling pretty satisfied with our situation.

Chemong Road store after renovations.

EXIT STRATEGY

At his age, losing Kent at Chemong, and seven years of Subway toil had left Shayne exasperated. So was I, especially with this twenty-four-hour animal I was trying to sedate. The monotony of sub-making made nine years feel like a lifetime. In addition, the unrelenting stress of operating a twenty-four-hour store, and we decided that we should begin to formulate our exit plan.

Meeting as a family, we decided to sell one of the stores and see if we could manage just one effectively. The easiest store to run was Chemong Road by far. It was newly remodeled, had excellent staff, sales were rising fast, and it wasn't open twenty-four hours. I would always lament, as the guy running Parkhill, that Shayne, the guy running Chemong, favoured the Chemong store and would insinuate that it was better operated than Parkhill. Our place was doing fine given its circumstances, but plainly, Chemong was easier to run with less demanding hours, a veteran staff, and a location in a cleaner neighbourhood, which meant fewer disturbances, if any at all. Couple that with the familiarity and comfort gained over four years of ownership and $150,000 in renovations, and this was clearly the ideal Subway to own. I would call it Shayne's Utopia. Therefore, Parkhill with its crushing hourly commitments would seem to be the logical one to sell.

The caveat with Parkhill was a sale before owning it at least twenty-four months was subject to a heavy tax burden. Shayne's Utopia, because we had owned it for more than twenty-four months, could be a tax-free sale, and easy to attract buyers because it commanded a lower sale price, seemingly more potential for growth, and it was a brand new store. We devised a plan where we would attempt to sell Chemong with Kent managing from January 2008 onward. He would transfer from the University of Waterloo to Trent for his final semester, and my parents and I would carry on at Parkhill.

We collectively agreed to sell Chemong first and vowed to put Parkhill up for sale after we owned it for twenty-four months. We were reluctant to sell our favourite store just after remodeling, but the plan seemed logical and we were confident the Chemong sale would be rapid and profitable.

So on November 14, 2007, we advised Mike Lopez that we were listing Chemong. It was no surprise that he liked the idea.

I continued to work on my relationship with Pineau, and it seemed to have a residual effect on Chemong as her compliance reports became more positive. We had also announced that we were selling the Chemong Road store, which coincided with the more positive reports. Meanwhile at Parkhill, we were spending a lot of money replacing equipment.

In 2000, an average Subway restaurant sold for $175,000, which was typically half of annual net sales. Building a new store and developing it ran at about $100,000. The investment is smaller but you start without a customer base. By 2007/2008, the average sale was $450,000 or 80% of annual sales, in large part due to the influx of Indian buyers.

While in 2008 it was only $175,000 to start a new store from scratch, there were very few start-up locations available. Resale meant instant entry, and all existing locations were coveted. Many sales occurred after vigourous bidding wars. And there weren't any Subway stores closing down that we had heard about.

So, in 2008 owning a Subway franchise was the closest thing to a "sure thing," which meant prospective buyers would be plentiful. With ENO listing stores for sale on their website and with word of mouth, it was unnecessary to advertise any further.

From November 14, 2007, when we announced we would sell, to February 21, 2008, when we accepted an offer that resulted in an eventual sale, we processed sixty-seven inquiries and applications.

SHOWCASING YOUR STORE

Selling a franchise requires as much preparation as buying one. The focus of the buyer is always on the sales, seldom on the profitability. Our school lunch business at Chemong was about $80,000 annually, although not as profitable as the regular business because these meals were discounted. With the average franchise sale approaching 100% of annual sales, the school lunch business became important, as did all catering. We pushed this end of the enterprise because it added to the sales total, resulting in a better final selling price.

Another important aspect of the resale is the actual showcasing of the store. Extra staff, extra cleaning, and extra owner-attentiveness are necessary once your restaurant is put on the market. Buyers who are interested will drop into your store unannounced and unidentifiable to get an idea of what kind of joint you are running.

Shayne would field all the prospective buyers' inquiries. He had a lot of experience and could easily tell the "live ones" from the "tire kickers." The primary question asked by the prospect was "how much is the rent and how long is the lease?" This question always irked my old man because it always preceded questions about annual sales or profitability, much more important topics for a buyer. Some high volume stores that have high rent are quite profitable because their food costs are lower than average and their sales are higher than most stores. From a revenue and expense perspective, each Subway's income statement will be different. The main focus should always be profitability. Besides, Subway transacts all leases and is very skilled in that area.

Sales at Chemong had grown significantly since our move. Renovation costs had exceeded $150,000 (the landlord had contributed $25,000). We set a sale price of $675,000, limiting a vendor take back to no more than 20%. Although the selling price was 90% of current sales, the renovation costs justified the price. We calculated that a new owner would receive a total purchase payback in forty months. There were many times during the pre-closing period that Shayne had second thoughts, because "Old age does that. Your brain is advising you to write cheques your body can't cash." Plus it had become his dream store, his Utopia, and to sell it was a bit emotional. But he remembered that owning a business isn't a love affair. He would say that he was twenty years too old to take this to another level. Youth needed to be served.

From the relocation of the Chemong store in July 2007, until its subsequent sale, we placed in the top ten on the Download Report almost every week. At one point, we placed in the top 3 in 40 out of 46 weeks. It would seem difficult for Pineau to mark us unfavourably when we were putting up these numbers. Needless to say, she found a way.

Sara Blake had applied for a job at the Bridgenorth store back in 2001. Hiring a bright, energetic, university student was always a no-brainer for us and she proved to be the benchmark for employees. When her sister Caryn applied, we saw, similar qualities and she would soon help anchor a pretty good line-up of sandwich artists. Quality employees are your greatest assets in an industry that churns through them constantly. The goodwill in any restaurant endeavour lies in the integrity of its staff. From the owner to the sixteen-year old trainee, customers will not return to a dull, inefficient, or unfriendly environment.

Positive relationships with employees such as the Blakes and others like them throughout our tenure made our time in the shop that much more enjoyable. Sara and Caryn lived in Peterborough, attended Trent University, and eventually followed us to the Chemong and Parkhill stores. When Sara graduated and moved with her fiancée to western Ontario, she successfully landed a management position with a multi-unit Subway owner.

It was not a great surprise when the Blake family became interested in purchasing the franchise. Parents John and Barb were longtime area residents and familiar with Subway through their daughters.

Although we did receive higher offers, this became the best deal for us, as both women could operate the store, John could do the accounting, and Barb could crack the whip. We accepted their offer knowing they possessed the crucial dynamic of being a family enterprise.

Family is the key prerequisite. However, the difference between the Randalls and Blakes versus the Shahs and Patels is that the latter don't have an end game. They are in this business for life, which is a quality that Ken Fielding and Fred De Luca look for in a franchisee. The Blakes would come to realize that fact as they too formed their exit strategy down the road.

The Blake sisters represented a dying breed of franchisees that did not possess the surname Shah, Bhalla, or Patel.

SELLING UTOPIA

The due diligence period upon closing the Chemong sale was uneventful for both the seller and buyer. The new owners already worked in the store and knew how to run it. Changes in procedure and staff were unnecessary. We finally agreed to a vendor take back of 25%, totally confident the store would be in good hands and all financial commitments would be met.

Kent's transition from Waterloo to Trent was smooth, he did a good job managing Chemong while Shayne, and I wrestled with the twenty-four-hour behemoth on Parkhill Road. Even with my efforts to placate and even entertain Pineau, her reviews at Parkhill, which were initially fair, became increasingly unreflective of our accelerated sales. After a year of ownership, we rose from 14th to 3rd (out of 230 stores) in sales as she continued to criticize our staff, our product, and even our hiring practices. It is rare when a restaurant sixteen years at the same location experiences a 22% increase in sales almost overnight.

Shayne really loved that store over on Chemong Road. It surely was his Utopia, in contrast with Parkhill, which had its share of complications. While Chemong kept bringing in the dough, Pineau continued to give passing marks on her reviews as she became aware of the future owners. She liked the Blakes, and it was no coincidence that the sale and transfer marched along in near record time. Sara and Caryn enrolled at Sub School ahead of schedule thanks to Pineau's efforts. The transfer would be seamless, as all staff would remain, and no break-in period was needed. We didn't even need to change the locks. It is very satisfying during a sale when all pieces fall into place the way they did in this instance. It's why we became Subway franchisees, to fulfill the "American Dream," in the footsteps of Mr. De Luca.

The sale to the Blake's had completed what was our one and only perfect scenario. Here's what happened:

Purchase from Cooks February 24, 2004	(192,500)
Profits to May 27, 2006	192,500
Renovations July 4, 2007	(125,000)
Profits: May 28, 2006 to June 18, 2008	220,000
Sale to the Blakes June 18, 2008	675,000
Net	**770,000**

So, you want to own a Subway restaurant? The Blake family will not regret the decision. However, don't fool yourself. For the Randall's, the aforementioned was that "once in a lifetime" situation. "Lucky bastard" strikes again.

CONFUSING EVALUATIONS

Before completing the Chemong transfer, Pineau needed to perform a pre-closing inspection of the store. As inspections are performed monthly, and she had done her previous one only a few days before, we assumed this final one to be only a formality. After all, it was virtually a new store.

Her first inspection after we purchased the Parkhill store should have tipped us off. Reminiscent of the thousands of dollars spent at Parkhill the year before, she forced us to replace the POS system and two microwaves before she would approve the transfer. Two weeks prior, things were fine, and suddenly we were obliged to spend another $7,000. The POS was functioning and the microwaves were working. In this case, we could have repaired equipment instead of replacing.

Upon completing the transfer, we bid farewell to Kent, who was training to become an urban planner, while my parents, Nolan, and I continued building Parkhill to prepare for its imminent sale in the spring of 2009.

As is the common theme, sales soared while our monthly reports continued to be poor. Barb would write about our inability in areas of customer service, food preparation, and bread baking. We were serving 14,000 sandwiches a month in a nine hundred square foot facility, on its own an impressive feat. We catered to a wide section of the community twenty-four hours daily and hungry people were flooding into our diminutive sandwich shop. After eight years of operating Subways, we thought we were running an efficient store.

There was no discourse following her visits. She knew our vehicles and would perform her "random" inspections when neither was present, thus avoiding any face-to-face discussion.

This pattern continued from August 2008 until we transferred the franchise September 2009, a thirteen month stretch where we were never marked in compliance. During this period, something happened with regard to the ENO Download Report. We were getting large sales percentage increases, and sometimes our name would be omitted from the report. When Shayne discovered that our sales increases were higher than the stores being named on the report, he called head office in Minden to inquire. He was advised to contact Mike Lopez about this situation. He sent Lopez and Pineau an email advising that our store had not been included in the report. Our sales continued to be in the top three until we transferred the store to the new owners. We were never offered an explanation of our omission from the reports.

On January 18, 2009, a city bus that had run a red light demolished Shayne's car. Luckily, he walked away. Two days later Pinot arrived to perform her inspection, unaware that Shayne was in the building working early that morning, with his unfamiliar rental car parked in the lot. Stunned at spotting Shayne, she exclaimed, "Why the hell are you here?"

PART IV

THE CUSTOMER IS NOT ALWAYS RIGHT

If you are not a people person, Subway may not be for you. Owning a Subway restaurant requires interacting with typical and atypical citizens on a constant basis. The clientele is eclectic, random, and comprises an all-encompassing demographic. Subway supplies a product that appeals to all types of consumers and, as a prospective buyer, a reliable brand. Without customers, there is no business, which is why we would strive to give them the best experience possible. The customer isn't always right but he or she is always deserving of the best service possible. We would never succumb to abusive or manipulative patrons because it sets a bad precedent and shows a lack of self-respect. The majority of people eating at our restaurants were a pleasure to serve. Others weren't.

One man would come in regularly, looking like he was fresh off the military base, or just fresh off the army surplus store. Either way, his orders demanded razor-like precision that, if not performed perfectly, would result in the type of intimidation usually reserved for a platoon. He was arrogant, delusional, and lived in his own world, the kind of guy you wouldn't want giving a speech at a wedding reception.

During one promotional period, we had a sale featuring any three six-inch subs for $9.99 with the only stipulation being that we would not give out stamps for the sale purchase. This man partook in the sale one evening and demanded that he be given stamps. When the stamps weren't given to him, he raised hell with Subway HQ and received a bunch of free stuff.

I later found out that he had spent some time in the army but never saw any action in combat. He had been delivering newspapers on his new bike for the past year, some kind of special model I was unfamiliar with, one he was proud to tell me he bartered off a young lad straight up for a pair of boots. He said it was the best investment he ever made. Then he told me he had lost eighty pounds riding his bike and eating foot-long Chicken Bacon Ranch subs for the past year. I directed my eyes to his midsection and saw evidence that contradicted the claim. Customers like this keep you entertained on an ongoing basis.

If you've watched enough episodes of The Simpsons, you are familiar with the Comic Book Guy. An overweight slob who scams little kids on what they buy at his comic book store and who possesses infinite knowledge of every mundane detail relating to comic books. Picture this cartoon in human form—even the voice—and you have one of the most infamous people ever to grace our presence when we were sandwich artists. This goldbricking superhero's costume consisted of track pants and a stained plain white t-shirt for each visit to our store, where his father who happened to showcase a prodigious toupee usually accompanied him. He could never make up his mind about what to order, relishing that he was making you wait for him. When we finally caught Comic Book Guy in the act of stealing fountain soda, Kent called him out. Comic Book Guy had nothing to say, just put his head down and poured out the soda. The dad, fresh off their weekly bowling game, said to Kent with a pensive smile, "I saw him doing that, and I was going to say something."

Another man would walk in our store, go over to the newspapers, and scan through them furiously while looking over his shoulder to see if anyone was watching, like a squirrel devouring a nut. When the coast was clear, he would grab the newspaper and run out of the store. As we were catching on to his scheme, he was becoming bolder in the acquisition of his favourite section.

Kent caught him red-handed and told him the papers were for customers only, the guy replied, "Nice way to treat your customers." Kent retorted, "You AREN'T a customer. You have never bought anything here."

There is no reason to let yourself be taken advantage of by customers. Don't fall into the delusion that all customers are benevolent and all-knowing. Many customers are totally wrong in their assessment of your restaurant. There are so many factors that affect the attitudes of customers that frequent your establishment. They might be drunk, on drugs, or angry about something else in their lives and choose to take out their angst on the person behind the counter. The important thing is to serve all of them with the utmost respect and give them the benefit of the doubt. When the odd belligerent patrons tried something like the guy who stole papers we wouldn't stand for it. The customer isn't always right but give them respect because they pay the bills.

KEEPING A CLOSE EYE

ENO is responsible for protecting the Subway brand, and they do so by monitoring their franchisees as closely as possible. One month in 2009, our original FC Steve Green, who was still operating in the area but who was no longer our current FC, was coming in to check up on us. He noted that one of our prices, the breakfast mega sandwich, of which we sold about one per day, was listed at ten cents below the suggested price. He came in two more times to make sure we indeed changed the price and restored order to the cosmos.

At one point in November 2008, when we hadn't seen Green in ages, he and his son suddenly arrived at Parkhill around midnight. Both were intoxicated. Customers and staff reported to Shayne and me the next morning that they were obnoxious, loud, and abusive. It seemed we had run out of their favourite cheese, and they were very upset about it. The two employees working were so offended by the Greens' behaviour that they woke Shayne up during the night to report the incident. Shayne dialed Green's phone number the next day and before Shayne had the chance to utter a word, Green exhorted, "I think we are blowing things out of proportion." It would not have been as insulting had Green actually apologized.

At one ENO meeting, I looked at the wine on the table and noticed the label read "Fielding" in giant print; he had brought it over from his vineyard. The wine demonstrated how his presence was always felt by the franchisees he was so closely monitoring.

He did not trust that they would blindly accept all that he and Subway would profess. As a safeguard against any questioning he and his staff would intimidate by speaking down to their audience and doing things like serving Fielding's wine at the meetings. As someone on the receiving end of those speeches, I was reluctant to voice an opinion because I was intimidated and fearful of the consequences of anything I said. Fielding created an atmosphere where discussion and discourse between franchisee and his staff was not encouraged. Instead, he wanted his franchisees to follow instructions in an orderly fashion. It appears that he doesn't think his storeowners have the knowledge or talent to enlighten him on any issues pertaining to Subway policy. He would prefer they keep their mouth shut to save him the time and keep things on an even keel. This may be a wise strategy, perhaps one that is used successfully by other development agents.

Now I don't know if all DAs have the same uneasiness about trusting their partners—the franchisees—or the same kind of inclination to monitor in such a fashion. They obviously need to have a keen eye on us, the question is how keen? Ostensibly, the purpose of their internal monitoring system is to ensure consistency among restaurants and is a big reason why Subway year after year is considered the best franchise in the world. Whether or not they are too intrusive when they want to be is debatable. The underlying message is "don't piss off your DA."

On a couple occasions during our ten years in the business, the marking of the stores became noticeably stricter than normal.

The first occasion was in the summer of 2004 after Shayne was approached by a disgruntled fellow franchisee. As I mentioned earlier, she was upset that the main FC for the area, Green, had a wife who was building a Subway in the mall directly across the street from her store without her ever being notified. Subway claimed she was sent a letter explaining the future presence of this new store, but she contends she never received such a letter. No other local franchisees were informed either. Angry that she was ignored and worried that the new store would hurt her business, she came to Shayne asking him to get all the parties together, including other local franchisees, so that everyone could be properly informed on what was going on.

Green and most of the franchisees in the area met at a local golf course for an open discussion. Virtually nothing was concluded other than what most had already known, that the wife of the area's main FC was constructing a new store in the mall. Green marked all of the stores in the area. He could easily mark his wife's store easier than the others. A couple months after that meeting, we had a new field consultant, Shane Menard.

By the summer of 2004, we were on probation. The strange thing was the store that he marked out of compliance was now in its fourth year with significant improvement made over that time. Sales were up; Green's previous reports had become very positive in comparison to previous years. Could that meeting have irked Fielding just a little? Why was Green replaced? The meeting had been a collective effort from all franchisees that had the same concern about what had happened.

When thinking back, Shayne recalled to me that it wasn't the first time he had held such a meeting. Through his experience as a dealer for Savin, quite often there would be dealer meetings conducted that would consist solely of dealers sharing ideas that would enhance business. Within a year of buying his first store, Shayne thought a similar exercise would be constructive when it came to Subway. A lot of decisions, when it came to what products to offer, needed to be agreed upon by all franchisees in the area. A good way to get those ideas in the air and agreed upon would be to have a meeting. These were decisions franchisees made on their own anyway so excluding Subway never appeared to be an issue. When Fielding found out that this meeting took place, he had a little chat with my old man telling him that you don't hold meetings on your own. That's not how things work around here. Shayne respectfully told him that he understood, that he wouldn't do it again, and that it was done with the best of intentions. The incident does beg a valid question: Does the franchisee have the right to do anything, even something as innocuous as this meeting was, on his or her own?

The Evaluation and Compliance Reports became decidedly more severe in our final year, 2009. We had bought our third and final store, Parkhill, in February of 2007. By the time we sold it, it had become the busiest store in the area. It was hard in the beginning, inheriting a new staff that had catered to the demands of the previous FC, Steve Green, and his marking criteria made it difficult. The changes I made, coupled with the new Pineau's requests, made it hard on a staff that seemed set in their ways. It wasn't until 2008 that I really felt comfortable with the staff and the manner in which the store was being run. I finally felt like I was getting a handle on running and staffing a twenty-four-hour store, which is completely different from a store open regular hours because of its staffing demands. To reflect those sentiments, Pineau was marking the store more positively. This ended of course in the spring of 2009.

The DA in every Subway region in the world gets marked just as the franchisees do, albeit not nearly as often. Someone from Milford is sent to evaluate the condition of a randomly selected group of stores within each DA's region. In the fall of 2009, we so happened to be one of those stores. It was discovered by the man from Milford that there was a mousetrap underneath our back sink of which we were unaware. At the next ENO operations meeting, Fielding criticized out an unnamed store for having a pest infestation and showed a picture of the mousetrap. You could tell from the picture that it was our store. The mousetrap was one left by the previous owners without our knowledge. Immediately, we hired a pest control specialist to inspect our store and he quickly deduced that there was no evidence of any rodents. Suddenly we were being marked out of compliance.

TWO RULE BOOKS

Subway produces an annual Operations Manual that covers, in great detail, every rule and regulation that governs your franchise. Throughout our time with Subway, ENO field consultants quoted from another manual we never saw. The FC would commonly tell us that certain rules are different in Fielding's territory. When we started at Subway, we thought we were running a franchise that required the consistent abidance of rules that applied to all stores across the globe. I guess it was a little different in this territory.

The OPS manual states that no employee is allowed to wear a nose ring despite the many cries declaring the rule a violation on individuality and personal privacy. Subway was lawfully permitted to enforce such a dress code. The previous owners of a store we took over both wore nose rings on a constant basis while working, and nothing was said. When we arrived, we were marked out of compliance three times for having females working with nose rings, even after we told them they weren't allowed to wear them. We asked our field consultant what the rule was. Pineau said employees weren't allowed to wear the rings. We explained that the previous owners wore them, and she said they should not have been allowed. This FC also marked the store of the man who ended up buying our final store. We met with this man one day at his store to discuss details of the sale. I looked over at his employees at work and three of the six had nose rings.

Shayne went to Mike Lopez and submitted an offer to purchase a second store back in 2003. Lopez did everything he could to stall the purchase, including asking Shayne to take the weeklong multi-unit course at Milford in the spring of that year. Subway requires that the multi-unit course be taken for those franchisees wishing to purchase a third store. Shayne called Subway HQ, and they told him that taking the course before purchasing a second store was a personal rule of Ken Fielding. Shayne submitted the offer to Lopez on April 29, 2003. He took the multi-unit course three months later, starting on July 27. The deal was dragging and by October, the store we were trying to purchase had gone up in value by $17,000, and we rightfully agreed to a new price, a price we could have avoided if it wasn't delayed so long. Finally, we closed the sale February 25, 2004, ten months after submitting the offer. Contrast that process with our final deal to sell our last store to Peter Shah. Shah submitted his offer to Lopez on August 20, 2009. We closed the sale September 23, 2009, only thirty-four days later.

We were marked out of compliance once for insufficient paperwork. Subway requires that the franchisee have the weekly paperwork from the previous four weeks available for the FC upon his or her arrival. As always, we had the materials in a filing cabinet beside the back desk, mere feet away from where she always sets up camp. This was during the thirteen-month period when she avoided Shayne and me. She asked an employee about the paperwork, and the employee did not know what she was talking about. The only people that dealt with the paperwork were Shayne or I and of course, this employee would have no knowledge of where the paperwork was located. Had Pineau called one of us, we could have explained that the paperwork was in the same place it was in every month. She had performed that exact task in the past.

Our FC had no trouble marking us out of compliance and ultimately forcing us to sell the store before we wanted to. She was capable of being as strict or as lenient as she wanted because it wasn't incumbent upon her to mark each store equally. Again, we didn't see her in our final thirteen months, which made it very difficult to avoid a non-compliance standing. Pineau's job was to help us in our day-to-day operations. Her mandate was to assist us, and she avoided confrontation for over a year. Those final thirteen reviews were recorded while she snuck in our door, leaving us unable to defend ourselves, or more importantly seek advice on the numerous topics we were concerned with at the time.

There were four areas that we had difficulty sustaining full compliance. The first was cleanliness, the most vague area to mark. The washrooms were her favourite topic of criticism. She would take pictures and describe how dirty these areas were. We would look hard at these pictures, unable to find anything dirty. My mother would come in every morning for two to three hours and clean, and she began to do this in our final year of operation. The improvement was noticeable to us in that final year.

The second area was glove usage. First off, I would like to say that I have been to a certain Subway, one marked by Pinot, scores of times since we sold our last store (yes, I'm not sick of subs yet), and they have yet to wash their hands in front of me before serving, a task that is demanded by Subway. According to the Subway Operations Manual, gloves need to be changed and hands washed in between every task. Before serving a customer, you must wash your hands in front of them with soap and water before putting your gloves on. If you are serving a customer and need to go to the back to grab something, you need to change gloves and wash hands before handling the item in the back and then again change gloves and wash hands before going back to the sub you are serving. This can become tedious and even trivial. Pineau marked Shayne out for grabbing cheese with the same gloves he was serving a sub with. When he brought the cheese to the front, he changed his gloves and washed his hands before he resumed making the sub. Because he missed that one step, where he was supposed to change gloves before handling the cheese (even though he changed them before he resumed making the sub), this was enough to mark us out of compliance. The rest of the time she was there, we practiced perfect glove usage and hand washing.

CUSTOMER SERVICE

The third compliance category we had problems with was customer service. In nine years at Subway, I am confident to say the best customer service practiced by our stores was in the final year, a period where we were often marked out of compliance. She would remark that we had certain customer complaints, that our staff would never give smiles and were constantly rude. We were never present to witness this dreadful customer service. She really had me worried because I took a lot of pride training and sustaining a staff that gave excellent customer service. Was she being honest? It didn't add up, but what could we do? I would have liked a chance to talk to her about it.

Our final store was situated in a low-income area, which was also a high traffic area. We had improved from 14th to 3rd out of 230 stores in sales volume. Running such a high volume store, we were going to get more customer complaints than the average Subway that did half our volume. Combine that with a rising unemployment rate and a floundering economy, which was the case in 2009, and you have more people looking for free food. We documented each customer complaint that was issued. The count had risen in 2009 based on the aforementioned factors. However, the percentage of legitimate complaints had decreased. Out of the complaints we received in 2009, 90% were unfounded and 80% of those, we had discerned, were comically ridiculous. Interestingly enough, the complaints filed under comically ridiculous (all complaints for that matter) were never refuted by Pineau when we explained what happened in each instance. She had no interest in defending our employees or us in these situations. ENO simply wanted the matter resolved, and even though it left us feeling isolated and neglected, it wasn't what bothered me the most. We could have lived with that. It was that she would continually refer to these complaints as an argument against our competence as operators. She never followed up on the complaints or tried to help us.

One complaint, which we filed under utterly stupid, involved a man claiming we had given him food poisoning. He contended that he should not have gotten sick when he purchased two foot-long cold cut combos (one of our most unhealthy subs) with lettuce, mustard, mayonnaise, and Italian sauce. He ate both foot-long subs—not a small amount of food—then immediately went to bed and woke up two hours later with an upset stomach. Crazy how that could have happened. He said the meat was bad. We would typically go through two hundred cold cuts set-ups a day. (Each set-up consists of a foot long portion of meat.) It was our most popular sub, and as a result, the meat was rotated constantly. When Shayne explained the story to Pineau, there was no response. Shayne went to great lengths to contact and explain to this particular customer the circumstances, and it was mutually agreed that food poisoning did not occur. The man admitted that he had eaten too much too fast and withdrew his complaint. In the consequent months, she would often refer to us having given this customer food poisoning.

We always aimed to follow Subway rules because we respected them. One rule that always inspired debate with customers was whether a foot-long sub could be wrapped as two separate six-inch portions. As small and harmless as this sounds, it incited a lot of anger from customers. Subway dictates you cannot wrap them separately if the person is only paying for a foot-long. The logic being that two separate six-inch subs cost about $1.50 more than one foot long. If allowed, customers could share a foot long, and chaos would reign. People will go to great lengths to save a dollar. A customer, unaware of the demands of a small business owner, would typically scoff at the denial of such a request. They would walk away thinking we were cheapskates. For this reason, I would commonly break the rule and wrap them separately, aware that this act of goodwill lost us profit. However, Subway initiated a more thorough secret shopper program where they ask these types of questions, so we began to stick by this rule.

One day a customer came in with his wife, who ordered the sub while he used our washroom before returning to read one of our newspapers. My mother was in the store and witnessed the whole event. At the end of sub-making process, the woman asked to have the foot-long wrapped in two separate portions, and the girl working politely explained that she wasn't allowed to perform such a task. The man walked over and began to intimidate the employee, who happened to be the most customer friendly employee I have ever been around in ten years at Subway. He demanded that the sub be wrapped in two. He said she was obligated to do so. The girl repeated that Subway would not allow us to perform such a task unless he was paying for the two six-inch subs separately. The man then asked her, "Do you know who I am?" He told her she was in big trouble and flashed his watch, which had a Subway emblem. He explained that he and his wife had operated a successful Subway franchise, this was no way to treat a customer, and he would file a complaint. He and his wife exited the store without making a purchase. The employee was embarrassed as there were a lot of customers who witnessed it. He eventually filed a complaint and word got back to Pineau who sided with the customer. My mother witnessed the whole thing and confirmed that the man was out of line. Pineau's response was that the rule could be bent, that it was not that important, and that this guy was a well-respected former franchisee.

Many of the complaints were incomprehensible rants from drunken people. One woman got her inebriated boyfriend to email us complaining two weeks after eating her subs that she was only able to choose from a selection of just three toppings. Two weeks had elapsed. Commonly our store would run out of a topping here or there, usually late in the middle of the night before our food order arrived. We had ten vegetable choices and four types of cheese. We would have had to run out of seven vegetable options. The email was a grammatical war-zone, and the points made no sense. She actually admitted to us later that she was looking for free food and that her boyfriend told her this would be a good ploy.

Maybe the most eye-opening incident was when a seemingly wholesome young couple with two young children ordered subs and proceeded to eat-in. My mother was cleaning out front when she noticed that the woman was changing her baby's diaper a mere five to ten feet away from the sandwich unit right out in the open. Shayne was also there and related to me that Beverly, as politely as one could do in such a situation, requested that the woman change the diaper somewhere else, perhaps their car. They complained that there wasn't a place to change the baby in the store. At nine hundred square feet, we didn't have that luxury. One can imagine the health standards being violated here. They complained, we contacted Pineau, and nothing happened.

Another person complained that we didn't have any mushrooms. Subway has never carried mushrooms on the menu. Every complaint was recorded and tallied. Most were unfounded, but as far as Subway was concerned, they counted in their records as a complaint. And those complaints contributed to us being marked non-compliant for customer service several times.

Another conclusion of all these complaints is that if Subway does not back their franchisees in these matters, stores are more susceptible to customer complaints. The age old saying, "The customer is always right," is false in many circumstances. When it comes to being bullied and manipulated by customers, that adage is dead wrong. When buying a Subway franchise consider that you may not get any support from your DA on this front, and that the word will get out that it is easy to get free food from your restaurant.

SECRET SHOPPERS

Secret shoppers are a commonality in the fast food industry. Their task is to arrive unannounced, perhaps buy a sandwich, and analyze the restaurant's performance on a number of levels. Sometimes these mystery visits were instigated by ENO and occasionally suppliers performed the function in conjunction with a product or promotion.

Most store owners are afraid of these people because they come in at random times to inspect the store on a number of levels, customer service being one of the main areas of scrutiny. Our perspective during our final years was different because we relished the opportunity for an unbiased analysis of how our store was doing. At the time, it was more random than an FC's inspection (in the sense that the secret shopper will not intentionally avoid the store owner) and infinitely more objective. After an FC review, the tendency in a store is to relax and not be as sharp as it was upon the anticipation of the FC's arrival. Days after a bad report from Pineau, a secret shopper came in during dinner, the same period Pineau liked to drop in to avoid Shayne or me. We were not present this time either. The secret shopper identified herself after doing her report and congratulated the employees on their performance. She rewarded the staff on duty with gift certificates.

Frito-Lay had a secret shopper program in the first quarter of

2009, and the Parkhill restaurant was targeted on three separate occasions. The results on such visits were not always shared with Subway franchisees but in the case of the Frito-Lay program, secret shoppers identified themselves at the conclusion of their visit, and on all three occasions, our staff was rewarded with praise and prizes. Where the scrutiny of an Evaluation and Compliance Review might have left our staff disenchanted, this would serve as a deserved boost for morale.

Eventually we received, in detail, reports from Frito-Lay for all three visits. The analysis was meticulous in its comparison to all other ENO locations, Ontario locations, and Canadian locations. Categories included:

- Restaurant details
- Cleanliness
- Product display
- Customer service
- Employee efficiency
- Suggestive selling
- Subway cash cards

Coincidentally, these particular areas were ones that Pineau had detailed us for being non-compliant.

According to the three secret shopper encounters from March 2 to June 22, 2009, out of the seven categories, we achieved 100% in six of them, 92% in the seventh. For all the categories combined, our average was 97.3%, the provincial average was 88.5%, and ENO's 230-store average was 89%. In customer service—our glaring weakness according to Pineau—we achieved 100% versus the provincial average of 93%. Combine that with our employee efficiency mark of 100% versus the provincial average of 96% and we were heartened with the results but confused with Pineau's contradictory observations.

EMPLOYEE SERVICE

Many of our employees were people attending the local university from other cities who had worked at Subway stores before, many of who were highly recommended by the owners of those stores. We felt very fortunate in this respect. They would commonly tell us that the FCs at their former stores were not nearly as critical as Pineau. When we defended our employees and explained that many had worked at Subways before she would say, "You got the bad ones." She would continually dismiss any defense against the criticisms of our staff. She would tell us that we didn't know how to hire people. Shayne had forty-five years experience hiring and firing. Our sales were up 22%, way above the ENO average of 3%.

Fred Deluca, the founder of Subway, had an idea a few years back and when he talks, everyone listens. He thought it would create a friendlier atmosphere if when a customer entered the store he or she would be greeted with, "Welcome to Subway." It was never introduced as a rule. The most current OPS manual explains that an employee must greet the customer or make eye contact within three seconds of them entering the store. Any polite greeting would do. "Welcome to Subway" was suggested by Subway but never inked in the manual. We would say it occasionally to customers who would undoubtedly laugh at us. It was a little hokey, superficial, and impersonal, but mostly customers thought it was funny. Suddenly Pineau was telling us to say this every time a customer came in. To my knowledge, we didn't have to say it and frankly, no one was comfortable saying it. I've been in plenty of other stores and not once has anyone greeted me with, "Welcome to Subway." When the new owners of the Parkhill store took over, she told them that they would improve their business greatly if they said, "Welcome to Subway" to every customer because we hadn't. However, Pineau's prediction was wrong as their sales did not increase, and I had scores of customers approach me after the sale complaining of the new owners' customer service. Customer service and efficiency are far and away the most important factors affecting sales.

CATCH 22

We were never given the tools to fix our problems and remain in compliance because we were never afforded the proper dialogue and in some instances denied the tangible materials (for example Barb Pineau's lack of knowledge in an area of Subway policy, which contributed to the withholding of a new oven and sandwich unit). We were criticized for not following protocol yet at the same time were denied the opportunity to get the one-on-one feedback required to fix those issues. It was a Catch 22. When you are marked out of compliance thirteen consecutive months like we were, and your field consultant has supposedly been an honest evaluator, it is only fair to say that such an operation would have to be so incompetent that the building would literally have to burn to the ground. This wasn't the case. What would Fred De Luca think if he knew there was a store operating that hadn't been in compliance in over a year under the same ownership but at the same time was having such tremendous sales increases?

The fourth compliance category we had trouble with was food quality/preparation, specifically temperatures. Restaurants are required to have their employees check and document each product's temperature in the sandwich unit twice daily. In the past when temperatures were too high, we would add ice or do something to rectify the problem while the FC was present. This would usually suffice, and we would not be marked out of compliance. Finally it was deduced that we needed a new sandwich unit and to purchase one ASAP to solve the temperature dilemma. Our sandwich unit was sixteen years old, breaking down, and needed to be replaced. It should have been replaced before we took over. Our FC wanted us to take temperatures four times a day instead of the required two stated in the OPS Manual. We were continually marked out of compliance because some days we marked them twice instead of four times.

After it was discerned we needed a new sandwich unit to solve the temperature problem, Shayne ordered and paid for one immediately. This was days after he was forced to sign papers that put the store under probation for being out of material compliance. This meant the store needed to be in compliance for six months consecutively, or we would be forced to go to a suicidal arbitration. Unbeknownst to Pineau—it is hard to believe she was unaware—since Shayne had signed the probation papers, the transaction for the purchase of the sandwich unit was being held in limbo. Therefore, the temperature problem could not and would not be resolved until that sandwich unit arrived, which it didn't for forty-five days. Eight days after signing the probation documents, she arrived for her evaluation and sure enough, we were marked out of compliance for temperatures, even though Shayne acted as quickly as he could on the matter. He emailed her, once explaining that the sandwich unit had been purchased and again to see why it hadn't arrived, even though his cheque had been cashed. She had no explanation. Of course, we were marked out of compliance for faulty equipment every month after Shayne sent the cheque, which was immediately after she had requested we make said purchase. There was absolutely nothing we could have done to avoid being marked out.

The same thing happened when Shayne ordered a new oven. The transaction was suspended because we had violated proba-tion. The oven finally arrived sixty-eight days after it was ordered, over a month after we sold the store. The installation cost was $997, a shade over the $64 Pineau estimated. And we were marked out of compliance for the imperfect bread we made because of our faulty oven, a problem that should have been averted. We would have avoided arbitration if the unit had been delivered on time. On most days, we would prepare and sell two hundred cold cut set-ups daily as they were our biggest sellers, which meant there was never any danger of them being in the "danger zone." Their shelf life is forty-eight hours refrigerated. We always sold them in twenty-four hours or less. In one Evaluation and Compliance Review, someone had prepared them—wrapped, labeled and dated—and set them in the fridge in twenty packs of ten. In the midst of these twenty packs of recently made cold cuts, which were all made at the same time that day, one pack was missing a label that had fallen off. The hungry price-conscious customers, whom they attracted, as they did every day, quickly consumed these cold cuts. One label out of twenty fell off by accident, and we were marked out of compliance.

Our last store: Parkhill Road.

PART V

THE END IS NOT SO NEAR

Shayne arranged to meet with Mike Lopez on November 6, 2008, to explain our decision to sell our last Subway. His relationship with Shayne had experienced an ebb and flow. Sometimes they concurred on things, other times they disagreed. The underlying factor though was a lack of mutual respect. Never in their relationship was there any trust. As a franchisee, Shayne was never treated like a customer, but like an adversary. Lopez and everybody working for ENO seemed indifferent to any success we had even though they had much to gain if we succeeded. By this time, we only saw Ken Fielding at the semi-annual operation meetings and even his appearances on those occasions had become fleeting.

In our decade with Subway, we remitted over $460,000 in royalties, and Subway in turn sent a percentage of that to Ken Fielding Enterprises. A pat on the back wasn't necessary, but it would have been nice.

It was time to call it a day and bring the Subway journey to an end. We weren't ever going to improve the relationship with the ENO. That had been proven. It had been our plan to sell after twenty-four months and that time was at hand.

When the announcement was made that we were selling Parkhill, Lopez breathed a sigh of relief, punctuated his approval by telling Shayne he was too old for this racket, this business was passing him by. It was a younger man's job, he said. I guess he forgot either that I existed or thought I was somehow in my sixties as well.

As much as it hurt to sell Chemong Road, it was a giant relief to know that the bizarre relationship with ENO would soon end with the sale of our Parkhill franchise. Driving home, Shayne was blind to the many more twists and turns that would occur before our sought after divorce.

ENO TURNS THE SCREWS

We were flushed with excitement in anticipation of selling our final store. I had been on injured reserve with a bad ankle for most of the winter but was now newly energized at the prospect of bidding the quick-serve restaurant industry adieu.

When the announcement that our store was for sale hit ENO's website, we were besieged with inquiries and visits from a variety of would-be purchasers. The very first suitor was Peter Shah, who already owned and operated five Subway franchises in the territory. Shayne had just returned from his Minden visit with Lopez when Peter called. They arranged a meeting concerning his interest.

It became quite evident months later that Lopez had alerted Shah to the availability of buying Parkhill the moment Shayne left that meeting in Minden. Shah owned the store situated in the building that was shared by ENO's Minden head office. All Lopez had to do after the meeting with Shayne was walk out the front door and see his friend Peter to inform him first hand, an act Lopez surely hoped would hasten our departure. Peter Shah met with us promptly and presented an offer. The price was somewhat embarrassing. It was $525,000, slightly more than half its value. Perhaps he knew he could simply play a waiting game until he was our only option. At the time, we figured there was no chance we would sell to him based on his initial price being so far off, and we had so many inquiries. Little did we realize that Lopez and company were pushing us into a corner and blocking our options.

Pineau marked us out of compliance once again triggering a letter from Subway Headquarters (HQ) terminating our franchise. In itself, this was not overly alarming, as this type of letter had arrived in the past and was always resolved if we were in compliance the next month, which we always were.

In December, Pineau did it again, marking us out of compliance and signaling dark days ahead.

As the New Year dawned and sales continued to soar above the Subway average, during a recession, Pineau would never mark us in compliance again. This was hard to fathom considering the store was enjoying unprecedented increases in sales in its eighteenth year of existence, and we were now in our tenth year with Subway.

FINDING THE PERFECT BUYER

While ENO scolded us during one of the most successful periods in our tenure, the news of our store being up for sale spread quickly, and suitors were lining up. They were doing so because we had a store that showcased well.

In January 2009, our sales were averaging $21,000 weekly—close to $1.1 million annually. The good news was that resales of Subway franchises had been averaging 90% of annual sales. The flip side to the coin was that we ran a twenty-four-hour enterprise. Because of our large volume of sales, our selling price would be almost double what an average store would sell for.

That was the down side to achieving such large sales targets. There would be less potential buyers because not many could afford it. In 2009, there would be many more potential franchisees that could finance a $500,000 purchase rather than a $1 million purchase. There were two solutions to finding the correct buyer. We would have to assume a substantial vendor take back and a twenty-four-hour operation was ideally suited for two families. We conducted our search for such a dual partnership.

The Parkhill store was our most difficult restaurant to operate. It tested our patience and stamina. Physically and mentally exhausting, the business pushed us to our limits. It was during this time that I understood why the previous owners, the Cleary's, had given us such a good deal. They had been at their limit, as we were now at ours. Through it all, though, one thing was as certain as the sunrise—it threw off a great profit, week after week.

Consistently we tallied a profit of $25,000 a month, almost 30% of sales. It was an ideal combination of high volume and low-fixed expenses. It was high risk but yielded high rewards.

So while Lopez was pushing us out, we wanted to get the right buyer, no matter how long it took. As each month went by, we earned another handsome profit, easing the negativity of Pineau's monthly evaluations. We set our price at $900,000, less than 90% of sales (at the time 90% was a common ratio for selling prices), but fair in the knowledge that it was harder to operate a twenty-four-hour store and buyers with $1 million in equity were a rare breed.

We received over one hundred inquiries. They continued even months after we sold the store. Even though ENO was disappointed with our operation, the public and prospective buyers looked at our store as a great business opportunity. Early on, it seemed evident we would achieve our selling price, as it didn't discourage the countless applicants visiting our restaurant and presenting offers. We had our tire-kickers, of course, but as winter rolled along, we entertained new parties on a constant basis.

There was no doubt that an Indian takeover of our Subway was a certainty. Only one of our one hundred plus applicants was not from India. And with the respect we had for our Indian friends, we knew that the lone WASP would never make it, although we didn't tell him so.

During January and February, we received four solid offers with deposit cheques. One was too low, and the others posed conditions we couldn't accept. Peter Shah phoned diligently and Shayne always accommodated him and politely asked him to raise his offer. As long as we were consistently receiving inquiries and profits were not abating, we felt time was on our side. Peter did increase his offer in due course.

Shayne reopened discussions with Peter who owned multiple stores in Northern Ontario. He had won franchisee of the year for the region, was a real golden boy with ENO brass, a very nice man who was a neighbour to ENO's head office. He had come to us immediately after we first put the store up for sale and offered us $525,000. Shayne told him we are asking for a minimum $900,000. He wasn't willing to even come close to the number we wanted so we said that's fine there is a lineup of people that leads out the door and around the corner that want this store that can pay the asking price. Between November 2008 and June 2009, we had eighty verbal discussions with prospective buyers, ten sit-down meetings, and six solid offers. It was just a matter of finding the right ones who could get the money together and could handle running the store. For these reasons, we were careful whom we selected, keeping in mind that we were willing to hold off until we got a buyer and a price we were comfortable with. We wanted to retire on a good note.

Something lingered in the back of Shayne's mind during the early part of 2009. We had received a termination letter the previous October, and Pineau would never mark us in compliance again. November, December, and January had now come and gone. Years before we experienced a termination notice resulting in an arbitration agreement. Shayne had forgotten the timing sequence of the event and while he wasn't overly alarmed, wondered why Subway had not followed up on their termination notice. It all seemed moot in the light of a pending transfer of our franchise. Shayne's premonition was that this was only the calm before the storm.

FAQUIR GILL AND VINOD PATEL

Faquir Gill, an Indian lawyer, had settled with his family in Toronto. He had acquired an excellent reputation for finding Subway franchises for sale and subsequently matching them with his Indian brethren. He kept in contact with Shayne over the years, and they became respected acquaintances. When Faquir learned our Parkhill store was on the market, he immediately contacted us. He charged a commission for his brokering and as we had many would-be buyers, we were reluctant to pay a middleman. He was persistent though and did have an impressive portfolio of potential investors. One such prospect was of great interest, and Faquir arranged a meeting.

In February 2009, a spritely Vinod Patel spoke to Shayne on the merits of his family purchasing Parkhill. Vinod owned and operated two successful Subways in Toronto. His aim was to relocate to a smaller community like Peterborough and enjoy its more calming lifestyle. A former actor in India, we became friendly quite quickly. He agreed that the manpower and the energy his extended family could provide would ensure success. We had a fruitful meeting that day and shortly thereafter, he made an acceptable offer, agreeing to our asking price of $900,000. The main condition was a provision of ample time to rearrange his affairs properly so that he could execute the transfer at a date that would allow him and his partners an opportunity to relocate. During March, he performed his due diligence, the offer was forwarded to Lopez, and we moved along, excited that our retirement from Subway appeared imminent.

It was too bad we were selling. We had set a sales record in March.

ARBITRATION

Finally, Subway HQ awoke from its slumber concerning the franchise termination letter they had sent to us on October 16, 2008, almost six months previously. We received notice that we could participate in an arbitration agreement that if completed successfully would result in our franchise agreement being reinstated. It had been a few years since we had gone through this procedure at Bridgenorth. Shayne requested paperwork from Headquarters. He was either ignorant, naïve, or just plain lazy, as he did not investigate the procedure and its outcome, as he should have. He figured he had been through the process before and came out clean so why not do the same this time around. He also thought with a sale transfer imminent, Subway should be reluctant to proceed as it could upset the increases in sales or heaven forbid an interruption in service from the Parkhill location.

The Subway operations manual is a tedious tome to read and comprehend, but reading it thoroughly would have made the arbitration/termination process clearer. And headquarters was only a phone call away to further explain details. Maybe Lopez was right. Maybe Shayne was too old and too presumptuous. We made a mistake in assuming the store would be sold soon. Even though an offer from Vinod Patel was in the hands of ENO for approval, it by no means meant this sale would be approved. Our assumption that we could sell before termination took place would cost us dearly.

To further lull Shayne into a complacent state, he received a phone call from Subway Headquarters. He had responded to one of the numerous surveys that HQ asks franchisees to complete concerning the performance of our local DA. Although Shayne had been critical of Fielding's methods in past surveys, no one had ever responded to his request for a return phone call or offered an explanation as to why Fielding was critical. Shayne poured his guts out for a good fifteen minutes suggesting improvements in how our DA, Ken Fielding, could improve his service. He also reported that we were about to enter into an arbitration agreement that was primarily prompted by a lack of communication with our field consultant.

The woman on the other end of the phone was quite empathetic and suggested he work with Subway legal to correct the situation. She urged that we contact Subway legal and sign the agreement when it arrived, and then thanked Shayne for his candor. The conversation concluded oddly though Shayne had mentioned that he was being forced to sell the franchise and pressured to get out of the business as Lopez had told him he was too old. He asked the woman if he should contact the ombudsman's department (a section within Subway Headquarters that objectively monitors the complaints franchisees have towards Subway) and ask them to examine our complaints about the treatment from our DA's office. She replied by stating that he had been talking with the ombudsman's office the entire time. This phone conversation emphasized the power that Fielding's office possessed. We always feared that if we complained to Subway HQ it would get us nowhere and furthermore, if he got wind of our complaints, Fielding might obstruct us further.

Against our lawyer's advice, Shayne and I signed the arbitration agreement. This would buy us time to complete the sale. After all, we had six months to establish the Parkhill Road Subway as being "in compliance" (or so we thought) and an offer from Vinod Patel was in the system. We sent the arbitration document to Subway

May 1, 2009, confident that other than some legal fees the franchise termination would not be executed. Moreover, our sales were running at 22% over the previous year, and it would be in everyone's best interest to continue building profits.

As soon as the documents had been mailed, Pineau arrived to perform her monthly Evaluation and Compliance Review. Five days had passed since we had signed the arbitration agreement when she marked us out of compliance for the tenth consecutive month. That number grew to thirteen before our franchise was transferred. This must have been a record.

After being put in line for arbitration, we knew we had to sell quickly before the case made it to arbitration. At least then, we could salvage something out of the store we had built up in value. We wanted to avoid coming out of these strenuous two and a half years with nothing.

Vinod was mysteriously being clogged up in the system. He was having difficulty meeting with Oddjob to expedite the application, and almost eight weeks had passed since we received and sent his offer to Minden. It didn't make sense that ENO would not at least make efforts to meet with Vinod considering they wanted us to sell.

Strangely, through the Vinod Patel interlude, no information was forthcoming concerning our arbitration agreement. Pineau continued to mark us out of compliance, but there was silence from Headquarters. Shayne decided to let sleeping dogs lie and focus on the sale of the store, which was ultimately more important.

It was now July 1, and the clock was ticking. We were still fielding inquiries for the store, as Vinod's application had still not been approved. A new engaging prospect and his partner entered the fray, and since Vinod's offer contained conditions we were not totally comfortable with, we decided to speak to the newcomers.

We needed a deal to back-up Vinod's if it backfired, and Jag

Nagra and Monty Kainth proved to be ideal candidates based on our initial meeting. Jag had previously owned a Subway, two families would be involved, and they offered a sizeable down payment of $500,000. They were willing to offer $925,000 ($50,000 more than Vinod Patel) and with a much-reduced vendor take back. In many respects, their plan had far more promise and chance of success than Patel's.

Lopez and Vinod were stumbling through the application/ approval process. After several weeks, and after Vinod's drop-dead date, July 7, had come and gone, we bid him and his offer farewell, putting us in a position to negotiate with Jag and Monty.

THE PRESSURE MOUNTS

Nearly eight months had passed since we told Lopez we were selling. We informed him and his boss that they would soon be receiving a fresh application.

Two events occurred in the first half of July. Jag and Monty made an acceptable offer that was quickly sent to ENO for approval and processing. Shayne then made the mistake of contacting Subway Headquarters to inquire on the status of the arbitration agreement. It served as a wake-up call for Subway. The legal department had been backed up all summer, and Shayne's phone call triggered an activation of the file.

We received a call from Subway legal shortly thereafter advising us we had breached our arbitration agreement when our store was marked out of compliance on May 5. Belatedly, Shayne engaged them in a conversation that was startling. Our understanding was that we had a month, starting May 1, when we signed the agreement to bring the store into full compliance. We were incorrect. The agreement, though not clear, was based on six consecutive monthly inspections where we were to be in full compliance. Shayne's heartbeat picked up as he finished the conversation with Subway legal.

Realizing that we had a limited time before the store would be terminated through arbitration, we accelerated efforts to transfer the store. Shayne had learned through conversations with Subway legal and the ombudsman's office that stores could be transferred during the arbitration/termination process, but he was now heavily relying on ENO's approval of Jag and Monty's application to avoid further complications of a sale.

Our meetings with Jag and Monty were encouraging and productive. We had investigated their credentials, met their families, and found them to be excellent candidates, capable of handling the stress of a twenty-four-hour operation. They were keen to start, intelligent, and had a solid financial base. Shayne phoned Lopez to advise him that Jag and Monty's application was of some urgency as Subway legal were closing in. Shayne's blood pressure rose once again, as Lopez guaranteed that said application could not be approved. He was unimpressed with a report from Jag's former DA.

It was July 28, and we knew that if we couldn't put the Jag and Monty purchase together we were in a deep hole. We were staring down at the abyss, and it did not look comforting.

Shayne explained to Lopez that Subway legal were on the case now, and we certainly wanted to end their pursuit by having a solid deal for the sale of the store. He agreed to meet immediately with Shayne the next morning. Usually meetings with ENO take a while to arrange so this was surprising.

THE LAST ROUND UP

As ENO's rebel made the one-hour trip to Minden, he kept reminding himself to keep his cool during the meeting, knowing that any confrontation would surely further compromise the situation. Some things were quite clear. Lopez alone could approve a transfer. He could suspend or at least delay Subway legal's termination process. Although transfers averaged twelve weeks from the application stage to the actual take over, Lopez could fast track the process.

When Shayne arrived in Minden, Lopez met with him immediately, unusual in that any previous visits to Minden usually involved a half-hour wait before he was acknowledged. Lopez's demeanour was calm and friendly, which was also surprising. Shortly after the pleasantries, he took the gloves off. He informed Shayne that he had spoken to Subway legal about our arbitration situation. Until then, we did not have a true understanding of how this process worked. He explained that an arbitration meeting would be arranged soon. The participants would be an independent arbiter, a representative from Subway legal, and the franchisees, Shayne and I. Lopez would also be present, representing ENO to present and confirm our non-compliance transgressions. He said that this meeting could occur at any time, without any warning, as soon as all parties could be present. He had only ten such events in his roughly fifteen years at ENO, and in every case the defendant lost, resulting in the complete loss of the franchise. In every case, he said, the franchisee lost everything.

Lopez, in essence, was saying that our operation was as bad as the worst ten operators they'd had in fifteen years.

Ultimately, he commented, when you signed the arbitration agreement, you admitted you breached the franchise agreement, and you were being extended the opportunity to be re-instated, if you were in compliance for six consecutive months. What he didn't say was that we were never given the opportunity to maintain compliance because Pineau was following instructions to block that opportunity.

He did most of the talking during the hour, which is impressive in a conversation involving my old man. He made it quite clear he was assuming control of the transfer of our franchise. He stated there would be no deal with Jag and Monty and proclaimed that there would be no "gold mine deal" for us; we were asking too much.

Lopez never divulged anything beyond the fact that the deal would never happen and that ENO would not even grant these guys an interview based on the former franchisee's reputation. They were Indian men with families that could help them run the store. Monty had owned a Subway before, and Jag had experience as a business owner. They were energetic, and the price was right, 92% of net sales. As soon as Lopez heard who was buying, specifically the one who previously owned a Subway, he told us the deal would never happen, that this guy owned a Subway and did something very, very wrong. Sufficed to say we were upset that he wouldn't give us an explanation or even at the least give these men an interview.

There had recently been a new DA appointed in London, Ontario, named Herman Grewal, who was quickly gaining a reputation as a no-nonsense administrator. One of his meetings (later confirmed by Peter Shah) included a speech concerning the fact that Subway resales were getting out of hand, price wise. The Indian influx was forcing prices too high, and the continuance of this trend would put franchises in jeopardy. These prices, he maintained, would put franchisees in a position where the stores could not provide enough profit to recover investment. Mike Lopez had become a disciple. A sale to Jag and Monty at $925,000 would be the highest price of any resale in ENO history. Lopez and Ken Fielding would not let such a sale take place, especially if we were the people enjoying such a resale.

"I hope you have a plan B," Lopez said, "because your time is nearing an end." Shayne told him he had another prospect. When he informed Lopez it was Peter Shah, the entire complexion of the meeting changed. He smiled and said he would have no trouble approving an application from Peter. The atmosphere had suddenly mellowed, and Lopez became almost father-like, telling Shayne that he wanted him to "leave with dignity," and he would personally work to complete the sale without debasing his integrity. Realizing that we had no impact on the sale of the franchise, Shayne told him he would immediately contact Peter Shah and see if we could pull this off quickly.

One phrase kept bouncing around Shayne's head on the drive home. "We want you to leave with dignity." Such a sentiment is usually reserved for those who do something wrong, he thought.

MYSTERY SOLVED

After the gun was pointed at our head, the next two months would be very stressful, as we had to find a new buyer who we could sell to quickly. We knew how slowly some of these deals were processed. It took Shayne ten months to close the sale of his second store after having a solid offer on the table. On the other hand, that deal was protracted because ENO didn't want us to buy. In this instance, we knew they wanted us out so they might try a little harder to speed up the process. All the while, we were communicating with Subway corporate about setting up a conference call to discuss the arbitration. We stalled as best we could.

Faster than you can say collusion, Peter Shah was at our doorstep. He and his wife appeared at our store within a few hours of Shayne's meeting with Lopez, obviously tipped by Lopez. He upped his offer to $700,000, with a vendor take back of $475,000 at 5.5 %, which I guarantee will be the best deal he consummates in his lifetime. The deal went down so smoothly and swiftly it was as if ENO had it planned all along. Compound that with the fact that ENO likes to go on their own sometimes, do things their own way. Steps could be bypassed. We stood to lose out on in excess of $225,000, based on the price we settled for and the price we had been offered from Jag and Monty. ENO was getting their golden boy to replace public enemy number one.

By August 20, Lopez had the offer on his desk and, of course, it was fast tracked like no transfer before or since. The turnaround took only thirty-four days. The following month we were put through the stress of not knowing if we would face the arbiter before or after the closing date of September 23. Lopez knew the outcome but was not about to assuage our apprehensions by letting us in on what was destined to transpire.

In these final few weeks, we learned much about the work ethic and good sense of the Shah family. Our experience with Peter and his family was positive and rewarding. He probably didn't realize that his fate as the future owner of our store had been orchestrated by ENO. I'm sure he thought he paid fair price, and the other suitors had offered way too much. After all, Lopez ensured him the price was right, the store being one that was out of compliance and not being run to standard. Peter was a gentleman throughout the process. He certainly came out of the process with his dignity intact.

We were now receiving calls and emails concerning an arbitration hearing scheduled for August 26, 2009, to be conducted by a phone conference call. Lopez was now being elusive in responding to Shayne's calls. Contact with Subway Headquarters confirmed that the transfer process for our Subway store was underway. As with many situations in the past, Subway and Ken Fielding Enterprises seemed to work at arm's length. The legal department that handled the arbitration didn't communicate with the transfer department. It seemed unnecessary to have an arbitration hearing when it would be moot when the transfer occurred. Lopez reported that, in all likelihood, the transfer would take place before the arbitration hearing. However, he could not say it with 100% conviction.

Under the guise that our lawyer was unavailable for the August 26 conference call, we were able to reschedule until September 16, a week before our proposed closing. If the closing was delayed at all, we were poised to lose everything. This was too much stress for a fiery sixty-seven-year-old who was promised he would leave with dignity.

We pushed Subway and Peter Shah every day in September. Final documentation was flawed, and we needed to drive back and forth to make amendments and get new signatures. Shayne drove about twenty miles north to meet me at a golf course I had just finished playing, so I could re-sign documents, such was the sense of urgency.

It was now September 15, and the conference call began with arbitrator Claude Thompson. Thompson was like a light through the fog. He understood that a pending sale would render arbitration useless and concluded that to avoid further expense, he would postpone the matter until October 23, giving us a month's window if the transfer were delayed beyond the September 23 closing date. His decision lifted a sizeable weight off our shoulders as an end was in sight. At last, we were confident we would be able to finalize the transfer before the grim reaper called.

From 2000 to the present, as the franchisees I knew were being replaced, the stereotype was that Indian newcomers were often difficult at the time of the transfer closing. It was reported that they would make new demands, refuse to honour items in the offer, or not meet the financial requirements.

At this time, the buyer is in a unique situation. The staff has been alerted, the seller has made plans, and the buyer perhaps only loses a small deposit if the deal is not consummated. Better to lose a $10,000 deposit than make a $600,000 mistake on a purchase that at the last moment did not appear right. Prices over the years had escalated, and Indian buyers were known as negotiators right to the end.

When we gathered to sell our final store on the morning of September 23, we anticipated that we might have some obstacles and were ready for any eventuality. To our delight, the closing was as smooth as any Shayne had encountered with Subway. All parties, including the much-maligned Pineau, were cordial and the event was concluded effortlessly.

Peter was so delighted with the deal, he presented both Shayne and I with a retirement gift. I got a 2009 Subway Convention wristwatch and Shayne a Subway duffle bag. I guess you could say we paid $225,000 for that gift, the discount Peter received on Jag and Monty's $925,000 offer. Subway's only farewell acknowledgement was the $35,000 expense that Pineau mandated before we could transfer the franchise.

We never heard another word from Subway or ENO as we faded into the mist. Not a thank you or a good luck. At least we had our dignity and our money.

SUCCESS OR FAILURE?

The difference between success and failure should be obvious and absolute. Ken Fielding Enterprises considered the decade the Randalls owned and operated three Subway franchises as an aberration, a fluke. They felt the continued increases that our stores achieved were based on luck and the attraction to the Subway brand. ENO had enough of Shayne Randall's in-your-face attitude and thought ENO's operation would be better served with different franchisees. Subway had selected the locations; the Randalls were interlopers, carpet-bagging, fast-buck, carney folk who didn't march to the Subway beat. Ken Fielding would say the Randalls failed in fulfilling the ideal of a compliant and subservient franchisee.

My old man and I view this through a different prism. Ours was a winding ride of ups and downs concluding in a financial windfall that, despite Lopez's success in minimizing it on our last sale, exceeded our goals. When your targets are met, it is time to move on.

EPILOGUE

Despite our experience with ENO, our overall experience with Subway was rewarding. This may be hard to believe, considering how we were treated and the resultant ill will Shayne and I share for Fielding and company, but there were a lot of good things to take away. I paid my way through university and Shayne's net worth in ten years went from the outhouse to the penthouse. We met some great people. My old man would probably say, "We had some great family time." If our relationship with ENO had been better, we would probably still be running stores. Therefore, it is imperative that you take out of this story that ours was a unique scenario. If you are lucky enough to find a store within the territory of a fair and honest DA, owning a Subway may be an enjoyable and rewarding opportunity for you.

My experience owning and managing our final store tested me mentally and physically, forcing me to develop certain characteristics I didn't possess before. It put some hair on my chest.

Subway is a great operation with a quality, health-conscious product. It offers a simple operation with potential for short-term and long-term profit and a sizable return on investment. Its brand awareness is among the leaders in the quick-serve industry and its reputation is outstanding. On the flip side, contractually, it is set up one-sided in favour of the franchisor, which gives the DA a great deal of control over who owns the stores in his or her area. Purchase prices are also rising.

From our experience, it is plain to see that generally a successful franchise or small business operation requires an efficient staff, excellent customer service, and a profitable financial structure.

Is Subway still the hot franchise? I would say yes but with a caveat. Purchase prices are rising which leaves less opportunity for a large return on investment. However, there is a great deal of long-term benefits. Once you own the store completely, have paid off all of your debts, there is a potential for high yearly income.

Franchising, you may conclude, is a rewarding venture. It definitely can be. You need to know the players, the risk, and have an exit plan. Surely, our DA Ken Fielding's operation is unique. Perhaps, our experience was as well.

One thing is for certain: Subway is no longer the "American Dream" but the "Indian Dream." And if you end up buying a franchise, you will have some stories to tell. I hope you enjoyed ours.

CPSIA information can be obtained at www.ICGtesting.com
Printed in the USA
BVOW071151080113

310092BV00001B/19/P